Map
OF THE
Western Peninsula of Ontario,
PREPARED BY THE
Credit Valley Railway Company,
shewing the
RAILWAYS COMPLETED AND IN PROGRESS,
September 1875.
Scale, 6 Miles to 1 Inch.
COPP, CLARK & CO. LITH. TORONTO.
LAKE ON
YORK
MARKHAM
Linton
King
Almira
Milliken
Weston
Eglington
TORONTO
ERIN
CALEDON
PEEL
ALBION
CHINGUACOUSY
ESQUESING
HALTON
NASSAGAWEYA
TRAFALGAR
NELSON
FLAMBORO EAST
FLAMBORO WEST
WATERLY
WENTWORTH
HAMILTON
BARTON
SALTFLEET
GRIMSBY
CLINTON
LOUTH
LANCASTER
GLANFORD
ONONDAGA
WALPOLE
PELHAM
GORE OF TORONTO
Orangeville
Mono Mills
Locton
Centreville
Columbi
Mellville
Paisley
Glasgow
Nanville
Charleston
Sandhill
Church's Falls
Claude
Cheltenham
Bellefountain
Rockside
Mayfield
Edmonton
Tuckers Mills
Grahamsville
Mount Pleasant
Osprige
Ballinafad
Brampton
Georgetown
Meadowvale
Mimico
Cooksville
Sprugside
Scotch Block
Hornby
Milton
Oakville
Bronte
Kirkwood
Burlington Square
Jerseyville
Alberton
Carluke
WESTERN RAILWAY
GREAT WESTERN RAILWAY
GRAND TRUNK RAILWAY
CREDIT VALLEY RAILWAY
CREDIT RIVER
ETOBICOKE
LAMBTON

Credit Valley Railway

George Laidlaw

Credit Valley Railway

"The Third Giant"

A History By
JAMES FILBY

1974
THE BOSTON MILLS PRESS

Number One, Credit Valley Series.

Published in Canada by The Boston Mills Press,
R.R.1 Cheltenham, Ontario.

The Boston Mills Press gratefully acknowledges the assistance of the Canada Council and the Ontario Arts Council in the publishing of this book.

OTHER BOOKS IN THE SERIES

The Boston Mills Press is a small independent Canadian publishing
house dedicated to printing local histories, collectors' handbooks
and other special appeal books. If you are interested in having
a book or pamphlet published, or wish to know more about us, please
feel free to write to the above address. We'll do all we can to help.

For Jean, a very patient and loving wife, who through many months of trying search gave encouragement and advice.

CREDIT VALLEY.
J.L. MORRISON

Builders photograph of Credit Valley Railway Engine #19 -*Canadian Pacific Railway photo*

"And from Chinguacousy's fertile plains
        We hear the thunder rally,
To open up wealth's thousand veins,
        Throughout the Credit Valley."

Poem by Alexander McLachlan, 1874
For the Credit Valley Railway.

EARLY CANADA WEST TRANSPORTATION

To a country with the physical shape of Canada, stretching thousands of miles from Atlantic to Pacific and settled on a relatively narrow frontier, cheap and rapid communication is an important requisite for growth.

The existence of conveniences of telephone and telegraph, radio and television, airline and superhighway, bus and turbotrain, makes it difficult to appreciate the immense inconveniences and hardships from the lack of such means of communication and transportation in pioneer days.

A simple thing like mailing a letter from York (Toronto), to England cost nearly six shillings in 1809, would take sixteen to eighteen days just to travel from York to Quebec City, the balance of the journey by boat as long as a month, and in many instances a two day trip over difficult trails was necessary just to post the mail. In 1816 there were but ten post offices in the whole of Lower Canada and nine in Upper Canada.

Great natural highways of lakes and rivers gave Canada a large advantage over many other parts of the continent in the earlier periods of settlement. Use of the waterways, was not without drawbacks, however, for in making their way to the oceans, these waters dropped from lake level to lake level, over cataracts and rapids, formidable interruptions. Long and arduous portages were necessary before the construction of canals and locks, and for many years, the birchbark canoe was the main mode of travel.

Even by 1826 to reach the sea, the traveller or export merchandise still had to portage, between Kingston and Montréal, the river barrier formed by the rapids on the St. Lawrence River. Similarly, a barrier existed at the Niagara River and once again goods or persons had to be transported while enroute to Detroit or the west.

But no matter how inconvenient the water routes were for long-distance transport, they remained for a long time the most important method of transportation. It became necessary to build roads, to supplement these avenues of travel, and, as settlements moved farther into the interior of the country and away from the shoreland of the lakes and rivers, the importance of land routes grew until it superceded the water routes', particularly for local service.

The roads of the Dominion were little more than cleared trails, and the rough grading, together with the logs thrown across the right of way to help prevent wagon wheels from sinking into the mire, gave rise to the term "corduroy road". The rains of autumn and the thaws of spring made the roads a mass of liquid mud and passage became only possible in winter when the ground froze or in summer when the sun dried it up. Even then a sudden storm made the roads all but impassable. By 1831, every male not listed on the assessment rolls was obligated to spend two days labour on the roads, and such labour was languidly performed, or, if possible, evaded altogether. Gillet, in his *Story of Canadian Roads,* states that Yonge Street was impassable in some seasons even after being macadamized a distance of twelve miles northward from Toronto.

From 1840 to 1850 numerous plank roads were built and Sir James Alexander, writing in *L'Acadie* or *Seven Years' Exploration in British America* (1849), tells in detail of the method of plank road construction:

> "The whole breadth of the clearing through the forest is sixty-four feet, the roadbed is thirty feet wide, the ditches on each side are eight feet wide at the top, two feet at the bottom and three feet deep from the crown of the road. The planking, on which is the travelling for rough-shod horses only, is sixteen feet wide. There are five rows of sleepers, four inches by six inches laid in the ground, the earth well rammed down on each side of them. Three inch plank, twelve inches wide, is laid on the sleepers and secured to them by spikes of iron, six and one-half inches long by three eights of an inch square. The road is graded to an elevation not to exceed two and one-half degrees."

Plank roads were thought to be a great invention, but, though satisfactory at first, they were generally a failure except as a temporary expedient. Soon turnpike roads or toll roads of gravel were common throughout Upper Canada and the controlling road companies were authorized to collect tolls from the users, in return for which right the companies agreed to keep the roads in repair. In general, the joint stock companies in charge of the highways left them in miserable condition. In spite of continual criticism, toll roads survived in some parts of Ontario well into the 1900's, with the last toll barrier disappearing as late as 1926. By 1841 there were about 6000 miles of post roads in Canada West, though their use was frequently difficult and sometimes impossible, and in 1850 some settlements in Canada West were still inaccessible by wheeled vehicle. Up to 1880 there was little or no improvement in the methods of road construction, and it wasn't until the Good Roads Association came into being in 1884 that proper standards were set for future road construction.

The Canadian stage-coach was a heavy, lumbering vehicle, and, like its counterpart the stage-wagon, was designed to travel the better road of the day. Travellers in the Canadian stage-coach were lucky if, when a hill had to be ascended or a bad spot passed, they had not to alight and trudge ankle-deep through the mud. If need be, they were expected to give aid when the coach mired or was unable to proceed under its own power. The stage-wagon consisted of a plank box mounted on wheels, with two or three wooden seats suspended on leather straps. The speed of travel was dependent entirely on the elements.

Travel by stage-coach in 1883 is vividly described by J.F. Pringle in his book *Lunenburgh, or the Old Eastern District* (1890):

"The author has still a vivid recollection of his first journey from Cornwall to York. He started from Chesley's Inn, then the Cornwall stage-house, about nine in the morning of the last Friday of January, 1833, in a stage-wagon. There was no snow on the ground but the road being hard-froze and smooth, good time was

made, and he arrived in Kingston stage-house between nine and
ten on Saturday night, where he remained until about seven in the
morning of the following Monday, when he started on the drive to
York, this time in a comfortable sleigh. He passed through
Napanee, Belleville, Trenton, Cobourg and Port Hope, and other
small towns, travelling continuously day and night until he got to
Bett's Inn, then the York stage-house, on Wednesday evening. The
journey, not including the delay of at least thirty-four hours at
Kingston, took about eighty-six hours. How would the present
generation (1889), who think twelve hours between Cornwall and
Toronto rather slow, like to go back to the travelling of the good
old days?"

THE COMING OF THE RAILWAY ERA

With the success of George Stephenson's "Rocket" on the Liverpool and Manchester Railway in 1829, a new "era" in transportation loomed on the horizon, and it was quickly seized upon by the early citizens of Canada as a means to make their lifestyle more endurable. (As will be noted later, within two years, Cobourg's citizens began to act toward the building of their primitive railway.)

As a means for opening up a new country for settlement, railways were incomparable: wilderness was converted into cultivated farms; direct and immediate connection was established between centres of commerce and afforded vitalization of the extremities of the country. It seemed all of these were accomplished without regard to weather or terrain, that the settler and the merchant were no longer totally deadlocked by the elements or the uncertainty of the water-travel and its many portages. The 'railway age' was at hand; it remained for the government to lead the way and promote its use. Unfortunately this took almost twenty years, while to the south, in the United States, the liberal policy of the U.S. government encouraged rapid railway expansion almost immediately after the trial of the "Rocket". A writer refers to the U.S. expansion in railways as "marvellous"; equally marvellous was the progress and development that followed. It is true that the early U.S. railways did not prove remunerative and, indeed, became a serious burden on the capital and industry of the country; their widespread failures and accompanying financial disasters became known as the "Crises of 1873". There followed a quietus to railway enterprise for a period of ten years which affected not only the U.S. but Canada as well. Notwithstanding the failures, the U.S. government again subsidized the railways by land grants and the issuance of currency bonds, and in the early 1850's the development of the U.S. railroads exceeded a rate of 3000 to 4000 miles of new lines annually. By 1875, their total exceeded 50,000 miles.

Several excellent volumes have been written which relate the details of the early efforts of the citizens of Upper and Lower Canada to bring about better means of transportation. A brief review of early railways, such as they were, will acquaint one with the era of 'railroading' prior to the charter of the Credit Valley Railway.

The first steam railway constructed in Canada was to carry stone from the wharfs at Cape Diamond to the Citadel of Quebec City in 1830. It was an incline railway operated by a stationary engine. Shortly thereafter, a fifteen mile railway, the Champlain and St. Lawrence Railway was opened on July 21, 1836 in the presence of the Governor General, Lord Gosford. The first train, consisting of two cars in which benches were placed and with no overhead covering, was pulled by a small engine and made the complete round trip of thirty miles in just one minute under the hour.

The first railway built in Upper Canada was previously a short portage road around Niagara Falls, from Queenston to Chippawa, built in 1839 although it received its charter in 1833. Known as the Erie and Ontario, it's grades were too steep for steam locomotives, so horse-drawn cars were used, but the railway proved of considerable value in the trade between Lake Ontario and Lake Erie.

By 1831, the citizens of Cobourg planned to build a line northward thirty miles to open up the back country. It was built primarily to haul vast amounts of lumber, together with grain and flour, from Peterborough to Cobourg harbour and thence to the United States by ship. The original charter is dated March 6, 1834 and the line was known as the Cobourg and Rice Lake Plank Road and Ferry Company. The president was Mr. William Webber, stage-coach proprietor and the prime promoter of the scheme. The road was built and successfully used for a short time, but, like most plank roads, it suffered the inevitable fate of upheaval by frost and the rigours of winter. With the passing of the Guarantee Act of 1849, a new era of railway building was inaugurated in Canada, and in 1852 the Cobourg and Peterborough Railway Charter was again obtained from the government.

The first sod was turned on February 7, 1853 and the complete line over the Rice Lake bridge was opened on Friday, December 29, 1854. Hardly had the line opened but the company was involved in difficulties; the first winter ice weakened the Rice Lake trestle, and the cost of the railway far exceeded that anticipated. Although the railway proved successful for the Port of Cobourg, it was a limited success. The bridge required almost constant repairs and the directors were continually in financial difficulty as a result. Sections of the railway as originally chartered were never completed and the line to Chemong Lake was never built, with the right to its construction being relinquished under the terms of the Charter in 1854 for non-usage. This section was later completed by the Grand Trunk Railway.

How large a place the Cobourg and Peterborough Railway took in the municipal politics of Cobourg may be easily imagined. For many years in-

sinuations and accusations regarding mismanagement of the line formed
the basis of elections. A sidelight of early railway financing is the admission
in 1858 by the Minister of Finance, the Honourable William Cayley, that he
had advanced ten thousand English pounds of public money to the Cobourg
and Peterborough Railway Company with whose President, Mr. D'Arcy E.
Boulton, he was related by marriage. Similar indefensible conduct, and on a
much larger scale, was characteristic of the financing of the Grand Trunk
and other early Canadian railways.

A final incident in the history of the Cobourg and Peterborough
Railway occurred during the early years of World War 1, when the rails
were torn up from the now abandoned right-of-way and shipped to France
where they were utilized behind the lines to transport ammunition and supplies.

RAILWAY ACTS OF THE 1800'S

The development of railways in Canada was greatly retarded by the unsettled economic conditions prior to the Rebellion of 1837 and the depression which followed. By 1849 only a few portage lines had been built but the Railway Act of 1849 gave a strong incentive to railway building in Canada.

The general Act, known as the "Guarantee Act" empowered the government to aid any railway not less than seventy miles in length by guaranteeing a payment of six per cent interest on a sum not to exceed one half the cost of the railway. In 1858 the government guarantee was extended to the principal, the government taking a First Lien on the railways so aided. Although the expectations of this policy were never fully realized, it nevertheless had the effect of giving a powerful stimulus to railway enterprise.

As a direct result of government attitude, between 1850 and 1853 fifty-six charters were issued and twenty-seven were acted upon. On May 16, 1853 the first railway locomotive in Canada West left Toronto and travelled to Machell's Corners (Aurora) over the Ontario and Simcoe Huron Railway. By 1860, seven years later, over three hundred locomotives were in operation in the province. Between 1849 and 1858 one thousand seven hundred and twenty-six miles of railways were constructed in Canada East and by 1860 there were ten lines of railways, some with extensive branches. By this date the length of railways in Canada West was one thousand three hundred and eighty miles, with most of the mileage accounted for by the two larger lines, the Grand Trunk and the Great Western.

In 1851 an Act of Parliament of Canada made provisions for the construction of a line through Canada West and Canada East. In the same year the Kingston and Montreal Railway Co. and the Kingston and Toronto Railway Co. were incorporated, both under the control of Mr. A.T. Galt and Associates. At the same time an influential group of English railway contractors appeared before the Canadian Parliament and persuaded a majority of members that it would be safer to entrust the project to them than to the inexperienced Canadian promoters. This company, Peto, Brassy and Betts, built the Great Western Railway and many other railways, and since most of the influential directors of the Grand Trunk were English, English Contractors were made the builders. The original charters were withdrawn and a new charter issued to the Grand Trunk Railway Company of Canada. An amicable arrangement was made with Galt and Associates, who became members of the company. Construction was pushed forward and on October 18, 1856 an announcement was made of the commencement of service between Montreal and Toronto. By 1859, the section from Toronto to Sarnia had been completed; the most noted contracting engineer on this part of the line was Mr. C.S. Gzowski, afterwards becoming Sir Casimir Gzowski (a memorial to him now stands on a section of Toronto waterfront park bearing his name). During the same period the section from Montreal was finished to Portland, Maine and other sections in Canada East were completed.

The Grand Trunk Railway was never a financial success. As usual in early railway building, the cost of construction was much greater than had been anticipated and the traffic on the line much less. Further, low business morality, prevailing in the early period of railway construction in England, carried over into the transactions of the Grand Trunk. While in control of the proposed roads and as shareholders, many members of Parliament used their offices to promote the development of national resources through railways. Public monies were advanced for ventures whose profits were shared by themselves and their associates. Several large fortunes were made in railway speculation by men in public office, with public trust; some even received titles from the Crown for their activities in railway development.

The misuse of public funds for the development of railway schemes by members of the government was a major contributing factor to the failure of the Bank of Upper Canada. The Grand Trunk Railway provides an example of railway speculation on a grand scale which ended in a failure so magnificent and completely disastrous as to lead to violent recriminations against its projectors and managers who were members of Canadian Parliament, and each and every person in any way concerned with the enterprise.

Defective organization, wherein the shareholders of the Company did not elect nor control the directors, where contracts were awarded without competition; where poorly constructed right-of-way resulted in destruction of rolling stock; where stations were poorly or improperly located; where there was extravagance in salaries and miscellaneous expenses; where probable traffic was over-estimated; where great inconvenience arose from the use of non-standard gauge between rails; all of these contributed to the demise of the Grand Trunk. In short, there was mismanagement of the whole enterprise of a staggering nature.

Economic conditions incident to the Great War of 1914 made the continuance of the Grand Trunk and its subsidiary the Transcontinental Grand Trunk Pacific impossible under private ownership. By 1922, both railways, together with the Canadian Northern, the Intercolonial and some other smaller roads, were amalgamated to form the Canadian National Railway System, which was placed under the direction of an independent and non-political board.

On the 6th of March 1834 an Act was passed by the Canadian Legislature to incorporate the London and Gore Railroad Company. Seventy-three prominent personages formed the corporators, among them Allan Napier McNabb (afterwards Sir Allan), George J. Goodhue, and Edward Allan Talbot. The charter was to construct a wooden or iron railway from London to Burlington Bay, as well as to the navigable waters of the river Thames and Lake Huron. Capital was fixed at $400,000 or 8000 shares at $50.00 per share with a twelve year limitation on the completion of the road and a provision for the doubling of the capitalization if the road were extended to Lake Huron. Nothing was done under this act and, as it was about to lapse in 1845, another Act reviving the first was enacted. An amendment was made at this time to change the name to "The Great Western Railway Company". Other amendments increased the capitalization to $6,000,000; the period of time to complete the line extended to 20 years and its routing to some part of the Niagara River.

From 1853 to 1856 so great was the speculation regarding the railways in Ontario that the demand for labour, timber and materials caused prices to rise as high as 50 per cent above original estimates. Contractors who had undertaken, one after another, to build sections of the railways at low estimates, failed, and the works had to be relet at advanced figures. An estimate made in 1852 for mainline work by one of the 'Great Western' engineers came about a million and a half dollars under the mark in 1854.

A sum of $3,850,000 advanced by the Government under the provision of the Main Trunk Guarantee Act provided the necessary funding to allow the Great Western to survive. By 1875 public money was being repaid and shortly thereafter the loan was liquidated. In contrast, the public funds advanced to the Grand Trunk and the Northern were never returned.

The Great Western, like the Grand Trunk, was originally built on a gauge of 5 feet 6 inches and was converted in 1869 to the standard gauge of 4 feet 8½ inches compatible with its connections in the U.S., the Michigan Central, The Detroit and Milwaukee at Detroit, and the Lackawanna on the Niagara Frontier. By 1875 the Great Western had, in addition to its own main lines, entered into agreement with or financed other lines throughout

Southern Ontario. These included the London and Port Sarnia Railway Company, The Canada Airline Railway, the Petrolia Branch, The Wellington, Grey and Bruce, the London and Port Stanley, the Welland Railway, the Galt and Guelph Railway and the Hamilton and Toronto Railway.

The Great Western later became a member of the vast array of small lines that ultimately formed the C.N.R.

George Laidlaw; *Mrs. Jean Shields photo*

GEORGE LAIDLAW THE PRINCE OF BONUS HUNTERS

Canada had many famous railway builders: Edward Allan Talbot and Sir Allan McNab of the Great Western; C.J. Brydges and William Molson of the Grand Trunk, to mention but a few. Among the most prominent and active in the Toronto area was George Laidlaw. His career began at Linassie, Scotland. He was the son of George Laidlaw of Comar, Ross-shire and the nephew of William Laidlaw, factor and one of the confidential servants of Sir Walter Scott at his residence at Abbotsford, Scotland. Little is known of Laidlaw's youth other than that he studied law at Edinburgh and later tried to join the Spanish Rebel Forces of Don Carlos. He was sent to Brazil by his family and was subsequently heard of taking part in the war between Mexico and the United States in 1848. With the lure of gold in California in 1849, the young Scot was next heard of making his way across the U.S.A. to become one of the "Forty-niners". When the gold rush ended, he returned to Scotland and remained there until 1855, when at the age of twenty-seven he emigrated to Canada.

Laidlaw was first employed in Toronto as a buyer for Messrs. Gooderham and Worts, and his success with this company prompted him to rent a warehouse and enter into business. About this same time George Laidlaw and a Mr. Middleton shared quarters in Toronto and Mr. Middleton's sister was invited to live with them and manage their home. Ann lived in Kirkdale, a suburb of Liverpool, and as quickly as possible emigrated to join her brother. George Laidlaw and Ann Middleton were married by Reverend Balwin of St. James Cathedral, June 10, 1858; Ann was twenty-four years old at the time. She died at the family home on Spadina Avenue in Toronto in 1886. Laidlaw was the father of five sons, George (whose interest in Indian archaeology was responsible for a substantial portion of the Royal Ontario Museum displays), Joseph, James, Charles and Harvey (who died in infancy), and three daughters, Katherine, Elizabeth Trout and Annie. George Laidlaw's influence in the area of Cannington is indicated by the naming of Trout St. after his daughter.

His experiences and contacts with other merchants and Toronto area farmers soon convinced him of the need for transportation by rail for the farmer's' produce in the immediate Southern Ontario region.

After carefully considering data collected from existing lines, Laidlaw was able to convince his colleagues that light, inexpensive railways would be satisfactory for use on local branch lines in Ontario, and since this was prior to the standardization of 1874, the gauge of three foot six inches was chosen. Forty pound rails were to be laid on cedar ties seven foot six inches in length, with a six inch bearing surface. The ties would be secured from the forests along the proposed right-of-way and low cost of maintenance and operations would be possible owing to lighter rolling stock.

The advantages of light, narrow gauge railway systems are outlined in the book *The Railways of Canada* by J.M. and Edward Trout (1871) and are summarized as follows:

1. the large comparative saving in first construction;
2. the large proportion of paying load to non-paying load or Tare Weight of the train;
3. the great reduction of wear and tear of permanent way, through advantage gained by light rolling stock;
4. the savings in reduced wear and tear of wheel tires from reduced weight on each wheel;
5   the large proportionate increased power of locomotives;
6. the proportionate increased velocities gained by the light system;
7. the greater economy in working traffic;
8. the compartive increase in capabilities of traffic;
9. the concentration of power, equilization of adhesion on all wheel flanges, reduction of wear and tear to permanent way, great savings in fuels and economy of wages for given power secured as gained by the application of the Fairlie system of locomotive engines.

Proposals for railways had begun in Upper Canada in 1830 but, as explained previously, until the Railway Act of 1849 was passed, it was almost impossible to finance any real undertaking. Two lines across the Credit Valley watershed area were under way in 1851 and were finished by 1856: the Hamilton and Toronto crossed through the southern area of the province while the Grand Trunk passed through Brampton, Norval and Acton; built prior to 1851, the Hamilton and Northwestern passed through Stewarttown and Georgetown and wandered across the southern and eastern part of Caledon Township.

Ann Middleton (Mrs. George Laidlaw); *Mrs. Jean Shields photo*

Prior to the publication of this book by Messrs. Trout, George Laidlaw had outlined all of these principles in a small publication entitled "Reports and Letters on Light Narrow Gauge Railways", printed by Globe Printing of Toronto in 1867. This piece of sales promotion material, distributed to the meetings held when the Toronto, Grey and Bruce was being promoted, explained in simple language the local people could understand,the features of narrow gauge railways as outlined by Messrs. Trout some four years later.

George Laidlaw was the moving force of the Toronto, Grey and Bruce Railway as well as the Toronto and Nipissing Railway. Both of these railways were started prior to 1870, with the T. & N. being completed and put into operation in 1872 and the T. G. & B. one year later. Laidlaw was also affiliated with the Victoria Railway. His prominence and influence in the City of Toronto was well established by his associations in business and clubs with many prominent citizens such as C.G. Campbell, John Gardner, John McNab, James L. Morrison, Angus Morison, William Arthurs, Robert Hay, John Baxter, William Gooderham, J.G. Worts, John Gordon, A.B. Lee, A.R. McMaster and E.B. Osler. The first seven of the aforementioned ultimately became the Board of Directors of the Credit Valley Railway, with George Laidlaw as its President, at the first meeting of its shareholders.

When Laidlaw was inspecting the proposed route of the Toronto and Nippissing Railway, he was very impressed with the land bordering on Balsam Lake, and first purchased land in the area in 1871 comprising five hundred and twenty-two acres. It was located on the shore of West Bay, Balsam Lake and was purchased from the widow of Rear Admiral Henry Vansittart of the Royal Navy. Vansittart, a cousin of Baron Bexley, came to Canada in 1834 and was given a grant of the above land by King William 4th; Vansittart was thus the first settler in Bexley Township, Upper Canada.

With the further purchase of adjoining lands, and several isolated parcels in the area of Bexley Township, including Ball and Hogg Islands in Balsam Lake, the estate had grown to 5000 acres prior to the time of his death. George Laidlaw named his estate "the Fort Ranch", although the name did not refer to any fort on the premises. A frequent guest, the Honourable Rupert Wells, as the times were very hard and money-tight, would ask his host on each visit if he were still "holding the fort".

In June of 1889, a short time before his death, a representative of the Toronto World visited him at "The Fort" and found the "one time Prince of Bonus Hunters" in good health and very involved with his land and his cattle. On viewing over four hundred prize cattle, the visitor remarked "You are a veritable Laird". "No, I am only a grazing farmer like my fathers were in Scotland, only I hold the fee while they rented their pastures" was the reply.

24

When the Laidlaw-Vansittart purchase was completed, the Vansittarts moved their home to another location and Laidlaw built two houses, one for his family and one for his servant's family, together with barns for horses and cattle and shelters for sheep plus a buttery. Later he supplied butter to the Queens Hotel in Toronto. Laidlaw began importing horses, cattle and sheep from Scotland and became interested in introducing good breeding strains into the area.

THE SECOND

ANNUAL SALE

—OF—

HORSES, SPRING COLTS, YOKE OF OXEN, COWS,
HEIFERS, STEERS, Thoroughbred JERSEY BULLS,
Thoroughbred DURHAM COW & BULL CALF,
SOUTHDOWN RAMS, Thoroughbred
COTSWOLD RAMS and EWES,
Berkshire Pigs, Goats, &c.,

The Property of GEO. LAIDLAW,

"THE FORT," VICTORIA ROAD, Ont.

Mr. ELIAS BOWES is favored with instructions to offer for Sale at

"THE FORT," BALSAM LAKE,

—ON—

Friday, 12th of October, 1883,

UPWARDS OF

100 HEAD OF STOCK.

Luncheon at 12 o'clock.   *Sale at 12.30 Sharp.*

TERMS:

Sums under $20.00, Cash ; nine months' credit on approved notes over that
amount ; or 7 per cent. discount for cash.

Sale Notice for Laidlaw Annual Farm Stock Sale; *Mrs. Jean Shields photo*

Laidlaw Homestead ("The Fort") 1900; *Mrs. Jean Shields photo*

A Mr. Scott was brought from Scotland for the task of building dry stone walls, similar to the "dry-moat" type found there. Hand-split cedar shakes were used in leveling and placing the stones which had been procured from the fields by means of stone boats, drawn by horses. The fence progressed at the rate of a rod a day and was so well constructed that even today portions of the three miles or so, surrounding fields and corrals or along the roadways are in a good condition.

Laidlaw retired in 1881 and settled on the property he had purchased from the Vansittarts on Balsam Lake. It was here that he died on August 6, 1889 at the age of 61.

When it was suggested after his retirement that he be granted the position of a Senator in the Canadian Government, he declined, saying "I would rather spend the rest of my life watching beautiful sunsets and sipping good Scotch whiskey than to waste my time for even one day in the Senate." A self-made man, George Laidlaw knew his worth, set his mark, achieved it and was satisfied with his success and the inward warmth such satisfaction can give. At his death, the Toronto press referred to him as "One of the strongest characters of his day. One of the epoch-making men in the commercial growth of Canada, yet he emerged from his railway enterprises a poor man. No man of his generation did as much for the material progress of Toronto as he."

THE CREDIT VALLEY RAILWAY: CHARTER, PROMOTION & FINANCING

On February 15, 1871 the charter of the Credit Valley Railway was secured from the Provincial Government for the construction of a railway from Toronto to St. Thomas, there connecting with the Michigan Central Railroad, and running north from Streetsville Junction to Orangeville, with a further branch line from Cataract to Elora. Named as officers in the original Act of Incorporation, George Laidlaw, C.J. Campbell, Frank Shanley, John Burns, H.P. Dwight, J.S. McMurray, Robert Hay, H.L. Hime and W.H. Beatty, became its provisional directors until the first meeting.

Having obtained the necessary Charter, it became the task of George Laidlaw and his fellow promoters to gain interest and support from influential persons 'of means' in the area of the railway's route. In Toronto, it was obvious that Laidlaw should enlist the aid of his past employers and of friends made in the grain business. The railway was planned into the Streetsville and Milton area, where fellow promoter William James Gooderham of the Gooderham and Worts group, had large mills and holdings. Gooderham was also a reeve of Streetsville, taking office in 1869 after a nine year tenure in office by John Street; Gooderham's influence was of immense importance.

In the Orangeville "Sun" of 1871 are several articles concerning the methods of promotion. A chronological listing of a few news reports indicates the success of the promoters and, in some instances, the apprehension of the voters. It is obvious from these articles that at this time the "Sun" was backing the railway and its promoters as best it could.

> May 18, 1871 ...The Credit Valley Railway is obtaining pledges of support from several of the municipalities interested in its construction. Streetsville is pledged to aid it to the extent of $20,000 and the town of Milton is to grant it a bonus of $30,000. Mr. Laidlaw is advocating the construction of the line with his

usual ability, energy and **perseverance** and 'having put his hands to the plow' he is not likely to turn back until he has secured the construction of the road.

June 1, 1871 ... STREETSVILLE BY-LAW - $20,000 GRANT PASSED COUNCIL: RATIFICATION EXPECTED AT THE POLLS ON JUNE 22, 1871.
June 22, 1871...RATEPAYERS CARRIED STREETSVILLE BONUS.
June 29, 1871...RATEPAYERS CARRIED MILTON BONUS.

On August 31, 1871, an excursion of Reeves, Councillors and others interested in the construction of the Credit Valley Railway took place on the Toronto and Nipissing Railway. This, another of the Laidlaw interests, was intended to give the excursionists an opportunity of testing for themselves the capacity and merits of a narrow-gauge railway, for it must be remembered that Laidlaw was still promoting the Credit Valley as narrow-gauge at this time. According to the "Sun" report, "the party enjoyed the trip highly and expressed itself well-satisfied with the narrow-gauge system. The trip made some supporters for the Credit Valley."

Not all was as rosy as the preceding would indicate, for on June 13, 1872, the electors of the township of Caledon, Chinguacousy and Toronto (later Mississauga) rejected the granting of a bonus of $80,000 toward the construction of the C.V.R. The "Sun" stated that "the majority of the ratepayers do not understand the value of railway communications or understand their real interest."

Undaunted, the promoters plunged onward, and on November 28, 1872 a report appeared in the "Sun" of a "large and influential meeting of the ratepayers of Caledon", held at Alton in the interest of the C.V.R. with addresses in favour of the project being delivered by Messrs. G. Laidlaw, K. Chisholm, A. McLaren, R. Meek, and Dr. Riddall, after which a resolution was unanimously passed pledging the support of the meeting at large to the granting of a bonus to aid the railway.

Andrew Taylor of Galt wrote that "The promoters of the road had little money but it was through a district in dire need of better transportation that the railway was built. Bonused from end to end, built around hills instead of through them to save money and often with not even the men's wages in sight, the railway was built through the townships of North Dumfries, including Galt and Ayr." Taylor's book, *Our Yesterdays,* further relates a story wherein one Scottish settlement had decided to vote down a bonus. "Mr. Laidlaw was went for in hot haste"(since he could speak Gaelic)" and speak it he did with such force at a little country schoolhouse, that every good Scottish vote went in favour of the bonus."

Whatever can be said of the style of promotion, it proved successful in the end, for the railway received bonuses (as reported in the *Engineering Magazine* August 20, 1880) which totaled $1,035,000 as follows:

City of Toronto..............$350,000
County of Oxford...........$200,000
County of Wellington.....$135,000
A section of Waterloo....$110,000
A section of Halton........$ 70,000
A section of Peel............$ 75,000
Town of Milton..............$ 30,000
Town of Brampton.........$ 20,000
Town of Streetsville........$ 20,000
Town of Ingersoll ....$ 10,000
Town of Orangeville.......$ 15,000

Besides these gifts, the towns of Ingersoll and Orangeville and the villages of Fergus and Elora agreed to exchange their municipal debentures for the bonds of the railway, Ingersoll to the extent of $30,000 and the other three to the amount of $95,000 each. As well as these sums, over $100,000 had been received as interest on these subscriptions, the amount being payable from the date of its being granted, while the sums could not be claimed excepting as the work was actually performed. The government subsidy of $3,000 per mile raised an additional $420,000 so that a total of $1,630,000 was subscribed of practically free donations. Thus the cost per mile of approximately $14,300 was reduced by $10,300 per mile in donations. The other $4,000 per mile had to be made up in extended credit from suppliers and investors, later to be paid back out of earnings. The original charter called for capital stock to the value of $140,000 made up of 1400 shares at a par value of $100 each.

The 'bonuses' of some of the communities carried a conditional clause that the new railway should never amalgamate or work in connection with either of the old lines in the area, the Grand Trunk and the Great Western. Indeed, such want of consideration exhibited by these two English companies for their Canadian interests caused some entire struggling communities to react and pledge voluntarily their monies to any person who had the courage to oppose the rich companies who had the monopoly of the carrying trade. The man with this courage was George Laidlaw.

Credit Valley Railway
TENDERS
FOR
Ties and Timbers

For bridges, delivered along the route of the Credit Valley, from Toronto to Ingersoll, and from Streetsville to Alton, will be received up to the 1st of November next.

Tenders for small quantities of Ties from farmers or others along the route of the railway; also tenders for ties and timber delivered on the ice on the Grand River above Fergus, and at the Forks of the Credit, are especially requested.

Tenders will also be received for a portion of the ties delivered at Carlton or Davenport Stations, and for the rails, posts and lumber required for fencing the line between Alton and Cheltenham, and between Milton and Ingersoll.

In case the bonus required from Centre Wellington is voted before the first day of January next, conditional tenders will be received for the ties, posts, rails, lumber for fencing, and bridge timber, deliverable as may be directed between the villages of Salem and Elora and the Forks of the Credit.

WORK BEGINS

The surveyors of the C.V.R. reached Milton on March 13, 1873 and were received by the Reeve of Milton and the Warden of the County of Halton. They were entertained at a supper at Wallaces' Hotel, where they announced to their hosts and visiting newspaper reporters that they had "found a suitable route from Toronto to Milton", and gave an account of the progress of the railway to-date. The hand of George Laidlaw controlled even the surveyors reports; he seized every opportunity to publicize the railway and to assure its supporters that progress was being made.

By June 12, 1873, the survey parties were under Mr. C.J. Wheelock, C.E., and were locating the line between Orangeville and Brampton; again Laidlaw chose to allow their reports to reach the press and to indicate that grading was almost finished from Toronto to Streetsville.

When July 24, 1873 rolled around, the station locations on the Elora branch had been designated and the report in the Orangeville "Sun" of that date relates the details with which they were outlined and the specifications within which the company had to operate in order to obtain their bonus. The following is an extract from these specifications:

Station Locations:
At the village of Erin, or one mile thereof.
In the village of Hillsburg, or one mile thereof.
At or near the town line between Erin and Garafraxa East.
At or within one and one-half miles of the village of Douglas, and should engineering or other obstacles cause the station to be located more than one mile from the town, the road to the village to be gravelled by the company to the satisfaction of the Warden of the County.
A flag station, with switch, located one-half mile from the Hines Hotel located on the Fergus-Douglas road.

A station within the limits of the town of Fergus located northwest of the Grand River.

A station within Lot 17 in the eleventh concession of the Township of Nichol and the Grand River in the village of Elora at a point west of a line between the 11th and 12th concessions of said Township and Irvine St. in said village.

A station within the village of Orangeville.

The company was also to be bound to erect and maintain free warehouses of suitable size and capacity at all stations with the exception of the station at the town line (item #3 above); also, to build and maintain workshops for this portion of the line in Fergus and to expand the line with the Wellington bonus pro rata per mile from a point between Belfountain and Elora to Salem.

Such were the precise limitations, and by October, 1874, it became apparent that the line could not be run through Belfountain. The shareholders were informed that "should the line through Belfountain prove impracticable, a junction at Church's Falls (Cataract) may be had under very favourable circumstances." The land in the Credit Valley area was to be preserved and a glowing report is given in the Orangeville "Sun" of May 13, 1880: "The Credit Valley Park, one of the most beautiful, romantic and picturesque parks in the Dominion, will be that now being surveyed by Mr. C.-J. Wheelock, P.L.S. for Mr. G. Laidlaw and occupying grounds along the western and northern branches of the river. If the views of the projector be carried out in full, as they generally are, this park will be a favourite of all lovers of the grand, sublime and beautiful in nature. Compared with it, the Victoria and Lorne Parks sink into utter insignificance."

A brief reference to Mr. Lumsden, the chief of the Survey Staff, in the Woodstock "Sentinel" of July 31, 1874 mentions that "he has gone to work on the Elora branch, the work upon the mainline to Ingersoll being so far completed as to warrant him in leaving its further prosecution in the hands of his associates." By reference to an article in the Woodstock "Weekly Review" and comparing the date of February 6, 1874 with that mentioned above, we can see that the surveying from Galt to Ingersoll took approximately six months. This same paper briefly mentions that the work crew on this section of the line were Italian and the majority new immigrants to Canada.

By 1874 the Province of Ontario had decided that in order to obtain a government grant or subsidy, a railway in future had to be built on a gauge of four feet eight and one-half inches. Prior to this time the choice of gauge was entirely up to the promoters of the railway and varied from 5' 6" to 3' 6" in width. The obvious problems of eventual interchange between railways can easily be imagined and it wasn't until the standardization of gauge took place that an efficient transportation system could be developed within the Dominion.

Therefore, in spite of his successful building of two narrow-gauge railways, the T G. & B. and the T. & N., Laidlaw constructed the Credit Valley on a standard gauge compatible with the major contemporary roads. Regardless of argument and design, operational proof taken from the above narrow-gauge railways together with the impending loss of subsidy due to the implementation of the Guarantee Act convinced Laidlaw and his associates that further ventures in the narrow-gauge field would be futile and the Credit Valley settled on standard track width.

At the annual meeting of the shareholders of the C.V.R. in Toronto on October 29, 1874, it was announced that the building of the railway so far had been done in a most satisfactory manner and the bridges at the Humber and Credit Rivers "if equalled are not surpassed in the Dominion" states the Orangeville "Sun". Full credit for the construction of the bridges is awarded to the skill of the Chief Engineer of the C.V.R., Mr. J.C. Bailey, who superceded Mr. Holt, his resident engineer, Mr. J. McCalman, and his superintendent of bridges, Mr. T. Watts. At this particular time the grading of the line was under way on the Orangeville and Elora branches, effectively

Sketch of Forks of the Credit Trestle 1879; *Public Archives of Ontario drawing*

managed by Mr. J.A. Walsh, while Mr. F.B. Brothers was in charge of the St. Thomas main line.

In order to gain entrance into Orangeville, Mr. Bowles, one of the directors of the railway, was successful in obtaining seven acres of ground on the property of Mrs. Ketchum, at East Broadway and East Fourth St. Mrs. Ketchum, with "commendable liberality", made a grant of the seven acres and gave the company the right to purchase additional land at the rate of $700 per acre when required. The site selected was one of the best possible considering both the interests of the railway and of the town. Even today it would lend itself as an ideal site for a terminal, with ample flat land for yard facilities — yet on the edge of town but close enough for passenger and freight handling with ease. The terminus consisted of a station and freight sheds as well as a turn-table, water tank and buildings for servicing engines, together with storage and side tracks. No trace of these facilities remains today save some roadbed and some concrete bases for watertower legs and engine pits.

By 1879, the construction of bridges had proceeded extremely well. A report in the February 14, 1879 issue of the Brampton "Conservator" carries a letter received from a resident of Cheltenham saying "We saw the engineer who is stopping at Mr. Henry's Hotel. He is about laying down a switch at the junction of the Hamilton and Northwestern road for the purpose of getting down there timber for bridges and etc. of which they have over three million feet ready for shipment as soon as the siding is down." This lumber was being brought into the general area so that bridges could be constructed, track laid and work trains moved over them and up the line toward Orangeville and Fergus.

On November 5, 1879 the first construction train arrived in Lambton Mills from Toronto and reports tell that the work is "being pushed forward with energy and despatch." Track laying was proceeding at the rate of one mile per day.

So interested were the people of the towns through which the railway was to pass that the newspapers publicized the shipment of the first freight. The Brampton "Conservator" of November 15, 1878 tells of "an earnest of the good things to come as the first freight passed over the line on Saturday last in the shape of a new stationary engine for the firm of P. & F.A. Howland of Lambton Mills. The arrival of the first passenger train is looked for shortly."

BRIDGES ON THE C.V.R.

A dramatic feature of a railway is its bridges. England had the "Firth of Forth"; New York had "Hells Gate", and the Credit Valley built two trestles that were a credit to the engineering of the day.

Frank Shanley, in his notebook on file in the Shanley Papers at the Ontario Archives, details the actual inspection of the railway for the Government on August 11, 1879. Beginning "Brampton, Ontario, 10 a.m. starting at mark in rail at station", he proceeds to chain the entire trackage working northward up the line toward Orangeville. His entries include "Commencement of trestle; 45 spans, 25 at 30 feet each and 20 spans at 20 feet each; bents on masonry. End of trestle; total 1146 feet." With these two single entries, he indicates the longest wooden curved trestle in Ontario at this time, one which the author believes is the record for curved trestle lengths in Ontario, with the possible exception of the wooden trestle and bridge leading to the ore docks at Port McNichol built in later years.

The Forks of the Credit trestle was 1146 feet in length and 85 feet high. It used approximately 500,000 feet of lumber and employed 250 men and 50 teams of horses. The teams were paid at the rate of $3.00 per day while Labourers received $1.00 to $1.10 per day. The Brampton "Conservator" of September 5, 1879 reports as follows "The Credit Valley Railway is progressing finely; about 400 men and 60 teams in the immediate vicinity of Cataract. The iron horse will reach Forks bridge on Saturday next." (September 13, 1879) This is the closest date of any reported information so it is safe to say that the Forks bridge was opened to work trains around this date. A further report in the same paper dated November 14, 1879 relates "A few lovers of sport of this village (Meadowvale) left by Credit Valley Railway on Monday for the Caledon Hunting Grounds near Kilmanagh. Business is dull this week owing to the bad state of the roads and the inclement weather. The passenger train which runs daily, is a convenience to our city. The C.V.R. station house at this place is nearly completed and work is progressing rapidly on a large storehouse." Since regular passenger

rks of Credit Trestle with Forks Station (upper right) 1879; *Mr. C. Smeaten photo*

service was in effect before November 14, 1879, our date for the completion of the bridge and first use is pretty well established at late September, 1879.

The trestle, built on a curve of nearly 90 degrees, crosses the western branch of the Credit River, allowing the railway to cling to the side of the narrow tortuous defile of the eastern branch. The river at this point is descending at the rate of 150 feet per mile but the gradient on the railway did not exceed 70, the consequence being that for a long distance up the valley on both sides of the trestle the road is benched out under the overhanging rocks of the chasm on one side, while far below on the other side, in the deep recesses beneath, the river foams and tumbles, affording some lovely glimpses of wild picturesque beauty.

C.V.R. Engine on Trestle at Forks of Credit 1884; *Public Archives of Ontario photo*

The other bridge which is unique to the C.V.R. was one which provided the railway crossing of the Grand River at Galt, Ontario. Since the Grand Trunk Railway had a branch on the west bank of the river and the Wellington, Grey and Bruce ran along a depression parallel to the river and less than a quarter mile distant from it, the C.V.R. was compelled to keep on a high level and cross both railways and the river sufficiently high to be clear of everything.

The Galt Bridge has five spans of iron together with trestling at either end. Over the Grand Trunk Railway is a Queen post truss of wood set within

Piers of Bridge over Grand River at Galt under construction 1879; *Mr. C. Smeaten photo*

Quarry Workers at Inglewood Quarry, source of the quarried stone for Galt Bridge; *Mr. C. Smeaten photo*

the trestling of one of the approaches. The whole structure, the first large railway bridge of entirely Canadian manufacture, was made by the Londonderry Iron Company, Nova Scotia, while the works were put together and erected by the Toronto Bridge Company. Since it was the first large bridge constructed of Londonderry iron, a series of tests were made on all the principal sizes at the Canton Bridge Companies' works in Ohio and repeated again in Toronto. In addition, most of the principal members were separately tested to a strain of 40,000 lb. per square inch, so that when a train of three sixty-ton locomotives was worked over the bridge at different speeds the deflection was less than five-eights of an inch in the centre of the span.

The total cost of the bridge and approaches including falseworks was $60,582. Its length was 900 feet and it towered 75 feet above the Grand River. According to the Galt "Reporter" of December 24, 1879, the first passage of a train over the bridge took place at 12:30 noon on that date, with Edward Toat in charge, locomotive driver Cross, chief engineer Bailey, assistant chief Ellison, section engineer Barber, foreman H. Fraser and an unidentified switchman. It proceeded as far as Barry's Cut and completed the crossing of the bridge, including its testing and official opening. The locomotives which made up the train were stopped on each section while measurements were made; then the entire train was backed up and run over the bridge once more at slow speed; then at moderate speed and finally at high speed, whereupon the bridge was declared safe and open to normal traffic.

In *Our Todays and Yesterdays*, Andrew W. Taylor of Galt, Ontario in 1969 recounts the first locomotive crossing of the Grand River Bridge at Galt on December 18, 1879: "Rather than risk human life in the test, the levers were set for slow movement and the crew jumped clear leaving it to cross the bridge on its own. At the far side it was met by other trainmen who climbed aboard and took over the controls." Since this story relates to the crossing of a single locomotive on December 18, 1879 and the official test took place on December 24, 1879, it seems quite possible that the 'story' really could have taken place as described and that the engine of the December 18 date really did check trackage, etc. and was the first to cross the bridge prior to the official test six days later.

A letter from the Chief Engineers Office of the C.V.R. dated December 6, 1876 describes the Humber Bridge as "having bridge timber of 14 x 14 pine as piers with the piers being carried down to bedrock." The bridge was over 100 feet from the bottom of the piers to the top of the rails. Ties were of white oak and the fence posts of cedar.

Another report, different in its description of the piers of the bridge, is in the Woodstock "Sentinel" of Friday, October 2, 1874: "On Monday

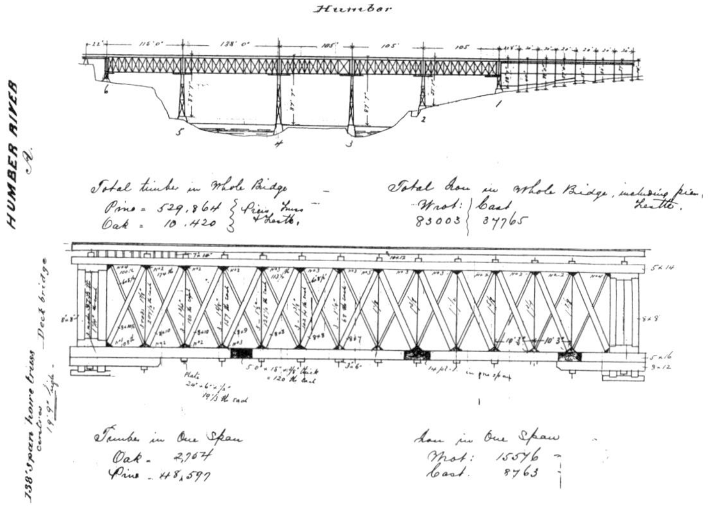

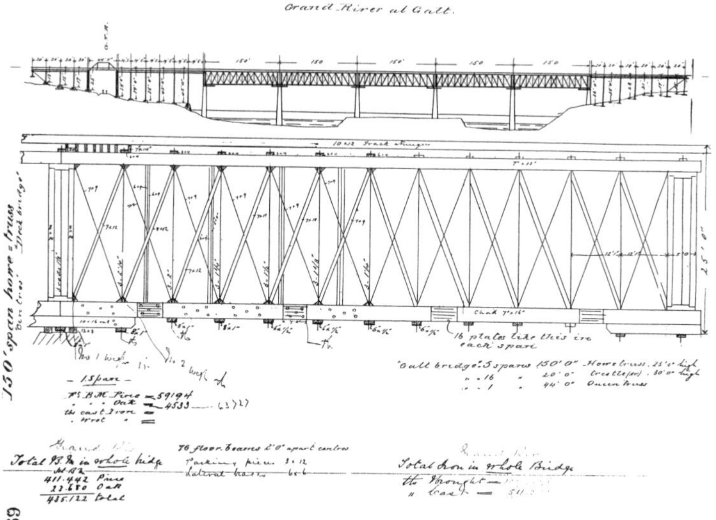

Humber and Grand River Bridge Drawings; *Public Archives of Ontario drawings*

morning a party started in carriages from Toronto for an inspection trip along the road. The first halt they made was at the Humber to examine the bridge across the stream. This structure alone gives the C.V.R. a certain prominence as it is pronounced to be the finest bridge of its description on the continent. The spans are built on the 'Howe' truss principle; one of 115 feet, one of 138 feet and three of 105 feet each, making a distance of 568 feet of truss at a height of 95 feet above the river. There are 800,000 feet of timber, almost 118,000 pounds of iron in the bridge and 3,186 yards of solid masonry in the piers supporting the spans."

The report goes into further detail and describes the Streetsville bridge over the Credit River: "This is composed of three spans of 'Howe' truss, 105 feet in length each and about 180 feet of trestling. The height from the water level is 36 feet."

The 1875 report of the directors of the railway tells that "there are now finished the Humber, Mimico, Pallett's Creek, Cooksville, Barber's Ravine, and Credit and Nith River bridges and 2174 linear feet of small trestling on the mainline and Credit and Meadowvale bridges and 1001 linear feet of small trestling on the branch line. Church's 'Overhead' and 'Millpond' bridges are also completed including fourteen spans of Howe truss. There is now erected 35 miles of fencing on the mainline, 17 miles on the Orangeville branch and 3 miles on the Elora branch. On hand are 56,017 ties and completed are 160 culverts and 61 pair of cattleguards on the mainline; 57 culverts and 19 pair of cattleguards on the Elora branch. An average of 620 men and 135 teams were employed during the season." The report details monies paid for the right-of-way, with a large amount donated to the company for wages and equipment, and also notes that a loss was sustained in trying to build a concrete bridge at Meadowvale. Adding to this loss was an overcharge for certain right-of-ways and some minor contractor failures. All of these totalled between eight and twelve thousand dollars. The directors' report further states that in 1875 "notwithstanding the loss, the company is in sound financial shape, but in order to continue would require a large government subsidy."

DIFFICULTIES AND CONTROVERSIES

Many vexatious delays and controversies occurred which seemed to make the building of the railway almost impossible.

In the Woodstock "Weekly Review" of July 30,1875, better than two whole columns were devoted to an exchange of letters between the Honorable George Alexander of Woodstock and the president of the C.V.R. George Laidlaw. Apparently Alexander objected to the C.V.R. trackage through his property and had indicated that he would take legal action against George Laidlaw personally. The attack was withdrawn later by a letter, stating that the reference was not "with your personal and private character" but "I could only be referring to your official management of this unfortunate enterprise."

Alexander warned that the route from Innerkip to Woodstock "will cause you to waste $10,000 of the bonus monies granted to the C.V.R. by the industrious inhabitants of the county." He further stated "you are not possessed of means to complete the work", referring to a portion of George Laidlaw's letters which mentioned that the railway would require more money than they presently had, but that they expected to get it. Alexander continued his attack by saying "Does anyone believe that the enterprise known as the C.V.R. will ever be completed? The general sentiment of the country is that its whole inception from the beginning has been a folly, and that the monies voted by the municipalities have been virtually thrown away. Who would ever purchase the bonds of a company whose line for nearly half its distance runs alongside one of the finest railways on the Continent, while no other portion of it is more than twelve or fourteen miles from other railways north and south of it?" Alexander's assumptions and arguments did possess some merit. However, the determined will of Laidlaw to see his railway completed led him to reply with an eloquence as can be seen in the following letter to Alexander:

The Honourable George Alexander,
Woodstock, Ontario.

Dear Sir:
    In reply to your favour of the 14th inst., I have to say that there was no course for the company to pursue other than to adopt the line recommended by Mr. Bailey as much the best and cheapest. We cannot continue the construction of the railway through your property without authority from a judge or unless we come to an agreement with you as to the value of the right-of-way. I have instructed proceedings to be initiated with a view to arbitration and to obtain the necessary order from a judge to enable us to work. We necessarily encounter a great deal of objection, reasonable and unreasonable, from proprietors of right-of-way, but either by private agreement or by the force of law we must go on. Since commencement of our work we have lost much time and money by the obstructiveness of the proprietors of right-of-way. The work from the Brock Road to Galt it is our intention to finish simultaneously with the Galt bridge, for which structural materials are being delivered this season. It is true we shall require more money than we have got to finish the whole line but we expect to get it. As to the statements and Affidavit which you say you will file against me personally, I can only promise that when they appear I shall defend myself against them to the best of my ability. The board of directors and myself regret exceedingly the necessity which sometimes arises for disturbing householders by the contiguity of the line to their premises; and in your case, if it can be proved that your grounds are a place of great public resort, we shall afford such facilities to visitors by the erection of covered platforms and etc. as will enable people, even from a distance, to enjoy your grounds.
    The value of your grounds will thus be very greatly increased; an important fact for the consideration of the arbitrators.

I remain, dear Sir,
Yours very respectfully
George Laidlaw
President, C.V.R. Co.

The attack had been blunted and a counterattack staged. It should be noted that no legal action was ever taken and the railway proceeded through on schedule.

44

The annual meeting of the Credit Valley Railway held on October 24, 1878 at Toronto relates another of the many problems faced and overcome by the dauntless George Laidlaw. While Mr. Laidlaw was in England a Mr. Angus Morrison occupied the chair in place of the president, and reported that "Mr. Laidlaw has succeeded in making provision for the completion of the railway. He had, after much opposition, concluded arrangements through Messrs. Saunders Bros. of London for the steel rail and fastenings sufficient for the whole line from Toronto to St. Thomas, Elora and Orangeville subject to the required bonuses and exchanges of debentures with the various municipalities. He has also concluded financial arrangements for the necessary rolling stock. A quantity of rail and fastenings equal to 5000 tons is on the way or has already arrived and is sufficient for the requirements of the company until the opening of the navigation in 1879. Tracklaying is proceeding two and one half miles west of the city and will be laid as far as Streetsville. Had it not been for the loss of the steamship "Copia" with 17,000 tons of rail and fastenings, Milton and Brampton would probably have been reached at the time of this meeting. The "Copia's" cargo has been duplicated."

Mr. Morrison further reported that the line between Woodstock and Ingersoll was complete and in operation and that the success with which this section has been completed "promises successfully for the whole undertaking." Laidlaw had written letters, travelled and spoken to the general public and raised funds in various municipalities and townships, enabling Laidlaw to go to London, England, to secure rail and related materials. There was tremendous opposition from the Grand Trunk interests which Laidlaw, with the Honourable Edward Blake, was able to surmount and only then obtain credit for the necessary supplies.

Further opposition appeared as even in the 1880's ecologists were attacking unnecessary destruction of trees, although then the abundance of forest was staggering and cordwood was an essential item, so essential that part of some bonuses to the railways was the establishment of rates for shipment of cordwood.

A September 9, 1880 newspaper reports "The C.V.R. is being fenced with barbed iron wire. The fencing looks durable enough, is a sure safeguard against snow build up and is cheaper than straight board fences or snake rail fences. The day is coming when such fences with heavier wire however, will be in use on all farms and the sooner the better. Drifts will then cease to trouble the chilly traveller and for cedar there will be found better use than splitting into rails. Try the wire fence and let the cedar grow." It was a requirement of building a railway in this period to completely fence the right-of-way with a four foot high board fence or cedar rail fencing consisting of split cedar rails five high. The first wire to be used on the C.V.R. was individual strand barbed wire either four or five strands high on cedar posts. In some locations three horizontal boards or split rails were topped by one or two strands of barbed wire. This combination fence was used where there was a possibility of pigs getting out onto the tracks. Near Inglewood and Cataract small sections of these board fences may still be seen today.

Early Snow Removal Crew on Elora Branch, early 1880's; *Vincent X. McEnaney photo*

Stories are told of the problems of early travel in Upper Canada, and it is fitting to indicate the need for snow ploughs, when we realize how primitive were the methods of clearing track. After a fierce storm north of Toronto, the entire route from Orangeville to Toronto would be blocked. Wedge plows were of no use and it was left to track crews to shovel their way north by hand. Mr. N. Weatherspoon, a superintendent on the Toronto, Grey and Bruce, relates that, due to narrow cuttings and inadequate snow-fighting equipment, two gangs of men living out of fifteen box cars spent six weeks shovelling their way northward from Toronto to Owen Sound. In the Forks of the Credit area, evidence of narrow cuttings may still be seen today and it is easy to imagine the snow falling and drifting until a solid wall of snow closed off any passage through the area. When temperatures rise above the freezing mark, the top snow melts; when the temperature drops again, the snow blockade is now surfaced with ice and requires the use of picks as well as shovelling.

The railways of today with their modern powerful diesel locomotives grind helplessly to a halt when confronted by overpowering snow.

The original basic patent for a rotary plow was taken out by a Toronto dentist, Dr. J.W. Elliott in 1869, but the railways were not interested. Thanks to the efforts of an Orangeville, Ontario, resident, Mr. Orange Jull, the modern rotary plow is capable of keeping even the remotest of mountain passes open all year round for passenger and freight movements. When Mr. Jull announced the development of a new plow representing quite an improvement and advance in principle over any other plow then in use, Mr. John Leslie, the Postmaster of Toronto, having obtained an interest in the new invention, arranged a demonstration in Toronto at the Parkdale Station of the Credit Valley Railway. Leslie Brothers of Orangeville built the first full-size unit and when the plow was ready to test, the season for snow had passed and it had all but disappeared. Nevertheless a gang of men succeeded by searching fence corners and other shady places and with shovels, brought forth enough snow for the demonstration. The rotary plow, pushed by a locomotive, pressed into the snow and the series of knives in the front of the plow, revolving at a high rate of speed, reduced the snow to powder and shot it out through a funnel over the right-of-way fence. The test was a success and from the modest rotary plow of the late 1880's evolved the enormous steel rotary plows now being used on nearly every major railway in the U.S. and Canada. The invention of the plow remains the honour of Mr. Jull, and credit for its first use belongs to the Credit Valley Railway.

The device needed refinement, and the Leslie Brothers built a new model from which the Cook Locomotive Works in Paterson, New Jersey built a working unit which was operated on the Chicago and Northwestern Railway in northern Iowa in 1885-86. By 1888 the Canadian Pacific Railway were building their own Elliott-Jull plows in the Montreal shops. By 1908-09 George Bury, General Manager of the western lines of the C.P.R., redesigned the plows and in 1911 the Montreal Locomotive Works produced a basic design for rotary plows used throughout North America with great success.

Labour problems on the railway are especially noteworthy. The Woodstock "Weekly Review" of July 23, 1875 reports that at Drumbo "On Saturday last the employees of the C.V.R. were paid and many of the men went to the taverns in the village and commenced to drink. When the liquor began to tell, a disgraceful scene occurred of disorder and rioting. About forty men were seen in all stages of intoxication. Fights occurred, for 'when wine is in, wit is out'. One man was nearly scalped, another had his arm broken, and it is a wonder lives were not lost."

The low wages paid to railway personnel at this time and slow payment of its employees resulted in frequent strikes. Spikers were paid 10¢ more than common labourers who received $1.00 per day. An advertisement in the August 1, 1879 "Conservator" of Brampton says "500 men wanted, wages $1.12; 200 men for ballasting and track laying $1.00 per day."

In the Shanley notebooks the salaries of train crews are recorded as follows:

    Conductors on mail trains......$1.80 per day for 176 mile trip
    Conductors on local trains......$1.80 per day for 130 mile trip
    Conductors on mixed trains......$1.70 per day for 85 mile trip
    Brakemen......$1.25 per day
    Baggagemen......$1.40 per day
    Enginemen......$1.75 to $2.50 per day
    Station Agents......$1.00 to $1.75 per day averaging $35.00 a month.

Early Hand Car (circa 1910) near Boston Mills; *Mrs. M. Belleghem photo*

At this time, Mr. Frank Shanley, one of the foremost civil engineers of the day, was in the employment of the Federal Government as an inspector. It was his duty to check the methods and materials used in the construction of the railway and, based on his reports as to completion of the work, the Government would release funds to the railway for further construction from the bonus monies allocated to the railway under the Railway Guarantee Act. A letter from the office of the president, George Laidlaw to Frank Shanley, dated September 8, 1879 gives a good indication of the financial problems which faced the railway and shows the situation as related to wages, etc:

> My dear Shanley: We are in a dreadful state for want of subsidy. The office is besieged by men with discharge papers, and overdue paper. The Grand Trunk is holding 50 cars of our rail for freight. We cannot move without money and we cannot get any on account of the state of affairs with the Consolidated Bank Note Company until we have your certificate for both sections. Bailey has just told me he thinks you will get out tomorrow. Will you please give everything else go by and settle this without fail. It is quite ready for you.
>
> Yours faithfully, George Laidlaw

The task of obtaining good men and keeping them must have been almost an impossibility when the wages were so low, and after having earned their money, the men were made to wait up to two months to collect it. It is possible that this 'employee problem' could have been a factor in the incidence of accidents which occurred on the C.V.R. until they were able to meet their financial indebtedness and payments were made on time.

Few enterprises ever encountered greater difficulties. Undertaken at the beginning of 'hard times', it was no small task to raise funds for its construction. Through the energies of Laidlaw and the generosities of the municipalities to be served by the road, each difficulty was overcome as it appeared.

LEGAL ENTANGLEMENT &
THE TORONTO ENTRY

Part of the entanglements in which the Credit Valley Railway became involved is dramatically shown by the Special Committee Report of the City of Toronto Council dated March 5, 1880, in which the Credit Valley Railway is seeking trackage rights into the city of Toronto and over trackage of the Northern Railway. The following is an excerpt from the report:
Railway representatives: Mr. Wells for the Credit Valley
        Mr. Darcy Boulton for the Northern
City Council: the Mayor and eleven Alderman
...Wells stated that the Grand Trunk Railway had obtained waterfront rights in a fair manner but the land which the Northern Railway occupy "I do not hesitate to say, was for the most part filched by them from the City, and their possession has since been maintained and extended with considerable skill." He also added that "the Northern Railway occupy a frontage of some forty or fifty acres without having paid the City one single farthing for it." Wells continued, saying that "the City of Toronto holds a license of occupation granted in 1853 of all that ground. That license was granted subject to the right of the Northern Railway to occupy, for the sole purpose of a terminal station, the land they then occupied but also subject to the right of other railway companies for the same purpose."

The Order in Council states, "occupation by the Ontario, Simcoe and Huron Railroad Union Company of such space as may be deemed necessary for them for the purpose of a terminus" and was dated December 9, 1853.

Boulton said that the railways (both the Grand Trunk and the Northern) only used land which the City abandoned, ie: the City obtained license of occupation for a continuous Esplanade from Berkley St. West to Queens Wharf but abandoned construction beyond Brock Street (not Spadina Avenue) and the railways occupy the area between Brock Street and the Queens Wharf.

When the Council was presented with all the various arguments, the map used by the Northern had apparently been drawn with one scale to show the Northern and Grand Trunk trackage and in a larger scale, magnified some three times its correct size, the trackage of the Credit Valley. The exaggeration of the Credit Valley claim was in fact due to the indication of the exact trackage of the Northern and Grand Trunk showing each individual rail in its exact location, while showing the entire Credit Valley proposed right-of-way over its whole width. The result was the appearance of a huge land request by the Credit Vallley Railway. The 'error' on the part of the Northern Railway, designed to make the Credit Valley Railway appear to be making impossible demands on Northern trackage, was detected almost immediately by the Council, and corrections to the plans were made. Such were the type of "smoke-screen" tactics thrown up by competitors to stop the entry of the Credit Valley into the City of Toronto.

Reference to the drawings of track plans would indicate an almost impossible task of trying to locate trackage rights for the Credit Valley in this instant, and to obtain the correct perspective of the reason for litigation. The Credit Valley had freight and engine facilities in the northeast corner area of the Dufferin-King Sts. intersection, and its main line extended down to the area to the northwest of the present Bathurst-Front Sts. intersection. The water terminal of the Credit Valley was located at the foot of Simcoe St., where a wharf was also available for transfer purposes. The main passenger terminal was the Toronto Union Station, shared by all the major lines entering the city. To simplify the problem, the Credit Valley Railway proposed crossing over all other trackage in order to obtain direct access to the main terminal and also to the Company's own waterfront wharf.

So complicated were the various routes proposed and so heated the arguments both for and against entry, that the entire matter was eventually taken up by the Railway Committee of the Privy Council in Ottawa. They appointed Mr. Frank Shanley to examine each of the alternatives and to report back with the best solution: one which would be the least objectionable to all parties concerned. On June 28, 1879, Mr. Shanley forwarded to the Committee a lengthy report wherein he said,"Having thoroughly, as I believe, exhausted the question and the different schemes proposed, I beg leave to report as having arrived at the following conclusions, the question resolves itself into not more than three schemes."

The scheme settled upon involved the following crossings:
1. The Toronto, Grey and Bruce to Queens Wharf...Three Tracks
2. The Northern Railway near Bathurst St...Two Tracks
3. The Great Western Railway at Brock St....One Track
4. The Northern Main Line on Esplanade St....One Track
5. The Northern on Esplanade St. (side tracks)...Six Tracks

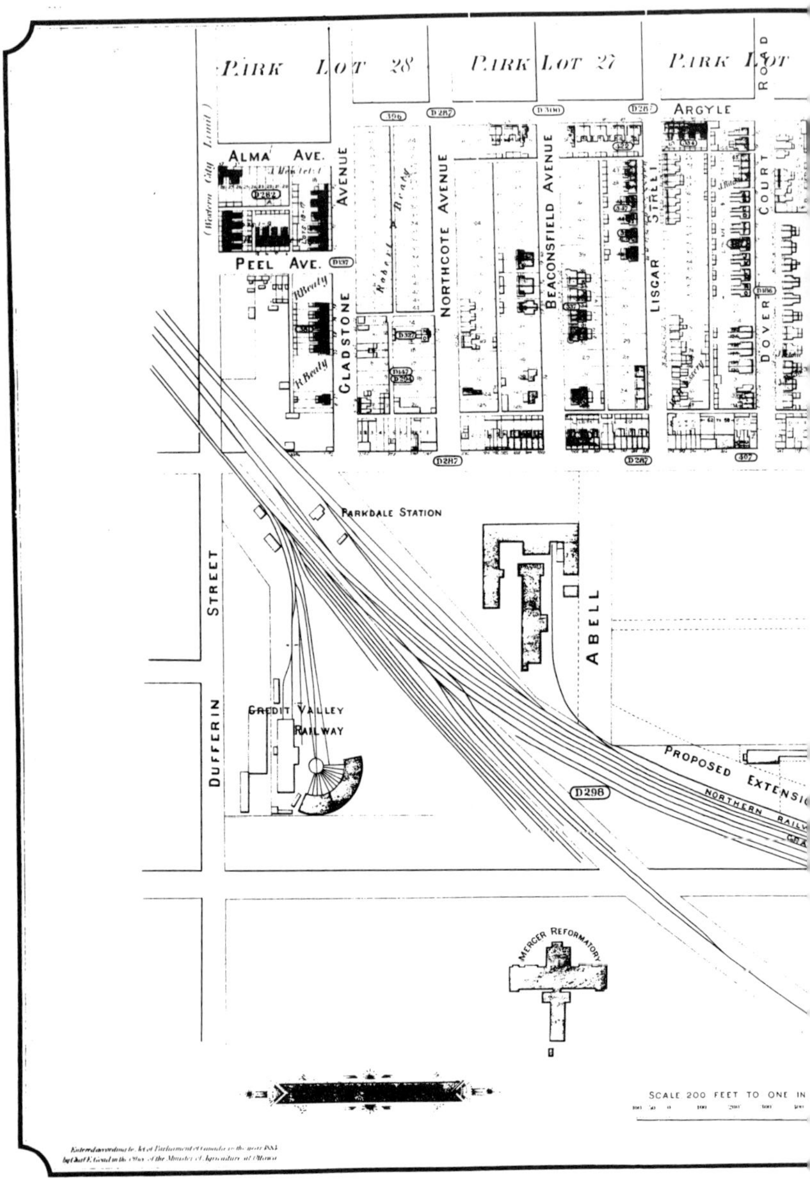

PARK LOT 28
PARK LOT 27
PARK LOT
ROAD
ARGYLE
ALMA AVE.
PEEL AVE.
Gladstone Avenue
Northcote Avenue
Beaconsfield Avenue
Liscar Street
Dover Court Road
(Western City Limit)
Parkdale Station
Credit Valley Railway
Abell
Dufferin Street
Proposed Extension
Northern Railway
Mercer Reformatory
D 298
SCALE 200 FEET TO ONE IN

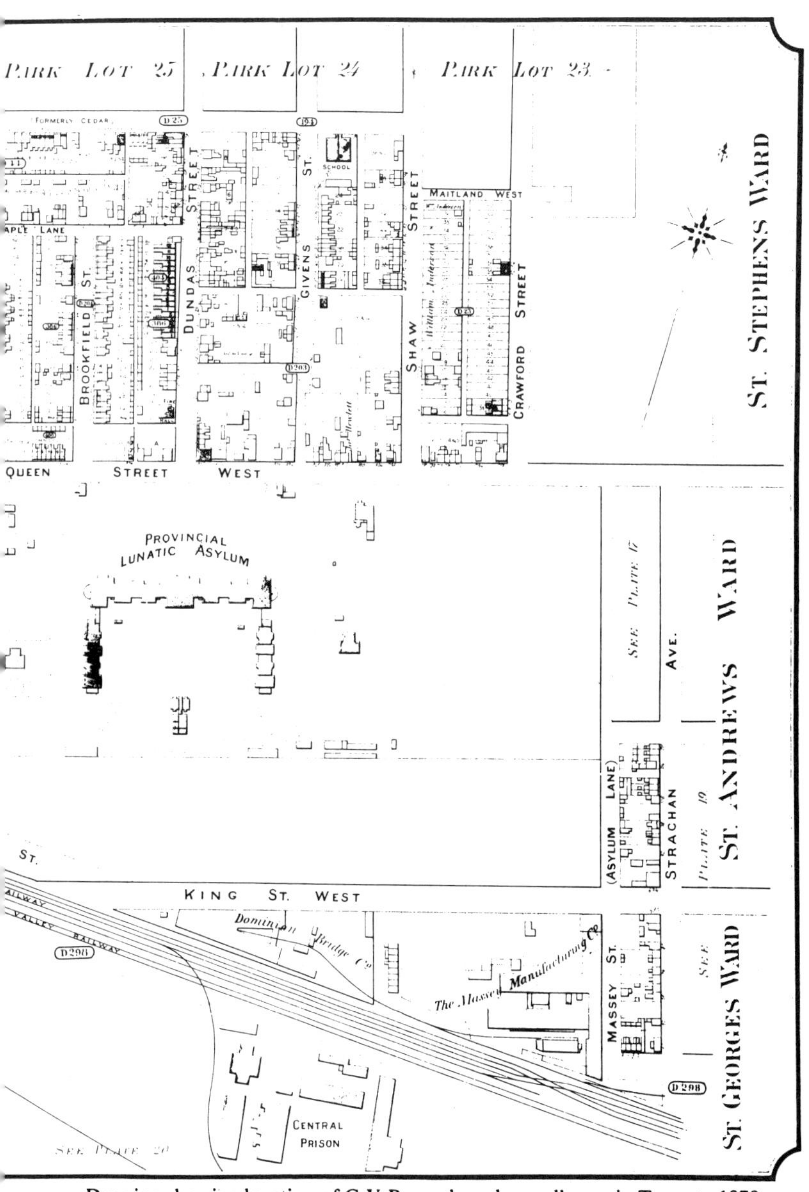

Drawing showing location of C.V.R. yards and roundhouse in Toronto 1879;
Toronto Public Library Map

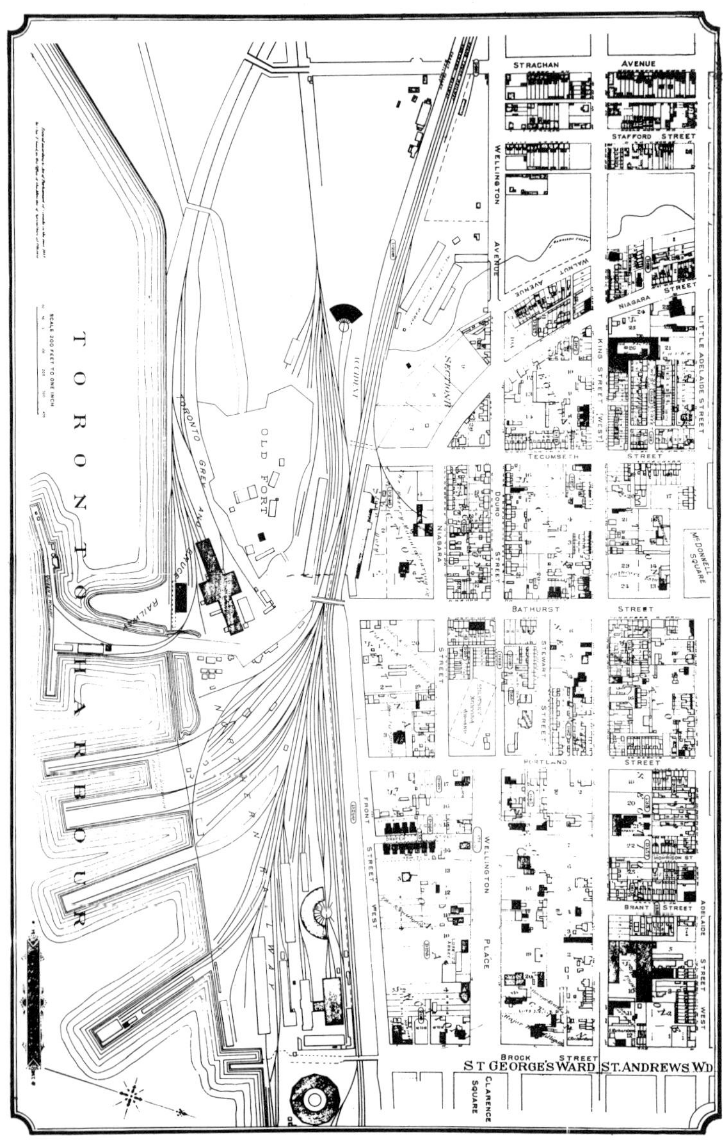

Drawing of Central Railway Area of Toronto, 1884; *Toronto Public Library Map*

The complexity of a crossing of thirteen tracks of three independent railways gives some idea of the chaotic engineering in the mid to late 1800's railroad era. The drawings show the general layout at the time of the problem and the ultimate trackage laid out to enable the C.V.R. to enter its waterfront terminal as well as the Union Station.

The matter was finally resolved by the Railway Committee in 1880 and trackage rights were obtained for the C.V.R. to its wharf and to the central station for direct movement of passengers without transfer of either passengers physically from one train to another, or transfer of engines from Credit Valley to Grand Trunk. We shall see what a serious problem this transfer of trains had become and the ultimate danger to life of the traveller.

On May 10, 1879 at approximately six p.m., a special car was returning from an inspection trip with the executive officers and some specially selected shareholders in the Credit Valley Railway. Because final arrangements for running rights into the Toronto Union Station had not been completed, the Credit Valley engine, which had taken the car originally from the interchange track near Carlton, placed the car on the interchange track and returned to the Credit Valley trackage.

The executive and members of the party were listening to a summation of the work schedules so far completed on the railway and were being given a progress report on work taking place to date. James Gooderham and George Laidlaw, the president, were discussing the eventual completion of the line with their honoured guests, while awaiting the arrival of the Grand Trunk engine to take their special car the balance of the way into the Union Station.

The Grand Trunk engine, proceeding westward toward the switch at the interchange track, gave the signal for a divergence of route from the main line to the interchange track. (Four short blasts on its whistle.) The switch tender, knowing that an engine was to pick up the special car, and hearing the whistle signal, threw the switch and lined up the track so that the engine entered the siding where the car was standing.

The engineer, James Cross, stated later that he did not know that he was to pick up a car of the C.V.R. at Carlton but rather that he was to meet a Grand Trunk train at Carlton yard. He denied sounding his whistle, a fact refuted by a number of outside witnesses, and he entered the siding at a speed of about fifteen miles per hour. Fortunately for all aboard the car, the engine was backing up, tender foremost, and the collapse of the tender at the time of the impact tended to lessen the blow. Even so, it resulted in many injuries to those on board, and in the case of James Gooderham and John McNabb, very serious injuries.

Both men seeing the approaching engine and attempting to jump at the time of impact, were thrown from the car onto a pile of ties alongside the track, Gooderham striking his head on the pile. McNabb fell on top of Gooderham and suffered a broken leg and serious internal injuries from which he recovered. Gooderham died of his injuries next day.

The list of prominent citizens of Toronto on board the special car reads like the Who's Who of the city...Wm. Arthurs, Mr. Walmsley, Mr. Pardoe, Mr. Suckling Jr., Mr. Charles, Mr. Houston, Mr. P.D. Conger, Mr. Beaty, Mr. Angus Morrison, Mr. James Gooderham, John McNabb, George Laidlaw and Dr. Fred Wright. When the investigation was completed, the Grand Trunk Railway was held responsible, but this was not of much help to the Credit Valley Railway, as it had lost one of its most important promoters next to Laidlaw himself...James Gooderham.

A letter on file at the Ontario Archives, dated May 30, 1879 from Crossfield Iron Ore Works, Whitehaven, England and directed to Mr. Frank Shanley states that "we are pleased to hear that you were not injured in the serious accident at Carlton." Further investigation reveals that the actual location of the accident was south of Queen St. and almost directly behind Old Fort York. As we have seen there was vigorous opposition to the entry of the C.V.R. into Toronto proper by the Grand Trunk and Northern Railways. The C.V.R., notwithstanding the opposition of these two railways, forced its way into the heart of the city, and trains which formerly could go no further than Parkdale now arrived and departed from the Union Station. The first train to complete the run into Toronto did so on Monday, May 17, 1880. The Toronto papers did not see fit to report this small event, but Orangeville, Brampton, Milton and Woodstock commented with pleasure that it was "a feather in the cap of Sir John A. MacDonald to grant by legislation that which neither the Northern or Grand Trunk would give under any circumstances. This is a boon much appreciated by the travelling public who have shown it by a large increase in travel. The usefulness of a railway that extends over so large and populous an area as the Credit Valley does, would be greatly impaired if compelled to stop outside the city limits."

Under a headline 'The Credit Valley and the Union Depot' the "Canadian Champion" of Milton, dated September 1, 1881 states "For the past few months, negotiations have been pending between the authorities of the Grand Trunk and the Credit Valley roads to make the Toronto Union Depot the terminus of the latter road. It has finally been settled and the change will be made on Monday next, the 5th of September. Upon which date the St. Thomas extension will be placed in operation. Through parlor cars will then be run from Detroit to Toronto. The terms for the use of the Union Depot are to be fixed by arbitration."

The same paper, dated June 2, 1881, says "The Credit Valley Railway Company have commenced preparations to build a new dock and wharf at the terminus of the road in Toronto. It promises to be of very large dimensions."

To have had a railway bring its goods down from the back country and be unable to deliver them to the water's edge was unthinkable in 1879. Ultimately, however, delivery of raw materials to dockside in Toronto was really not as important as the promoters of the railway believed. Shortsightedness on the part of the planners was evident on two major counts: first, the extension of rail lines both east and west should have made the interchange more marked than it was, and second, the advent of steam-powered mills in the large centres, together with better roads into those centres, indicated the eventual decline of the railways as the great benefactor to the settler and the farmer. However, for the time being, rail was 'King' and access to a Toronto wharf was imperative. Access had been obtained and service could now be completed from Elora, Orangeville and St. Thomas directly into the heart of the City of Toronto. The Credit Valley Railway had been completed.

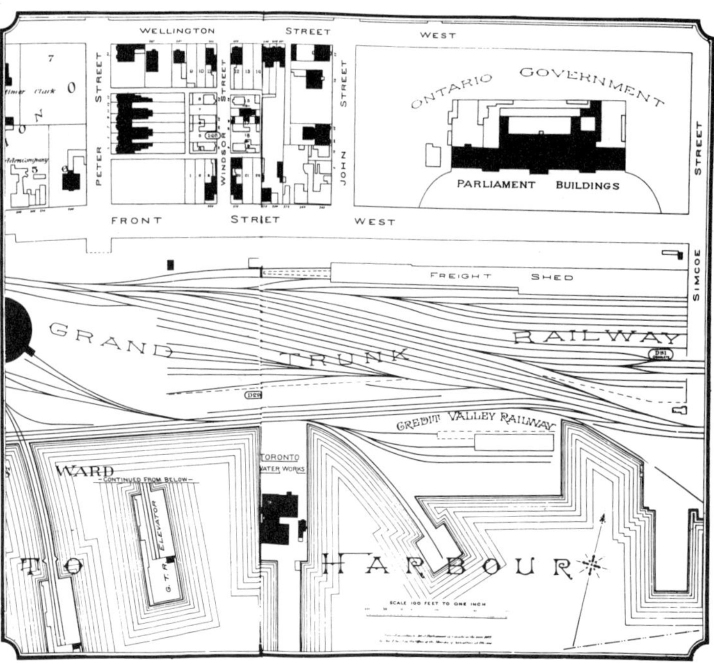

Location Map of Credit Valley Railway Docks in Toronto, 1884; *Toronto Public Library Map*

The Official Opening of The Credit Valley Railway at Milton, Ontario

OPENING THE LINE

The Credit Valley Railway was formally opened by his His Excellency, the Marquis of Lorne, Governor General of Canada at Milton, Ontario on September 19, 1879. From the charter to the first official train it took eight years. The railway building had been hampered by lack of funds, opposed by the existing railways in obtaining credit, further burdened by a strike of its employees in the Toronto area in 1880, and lengthy litigation to obtain entry into the City of Toronto. Opening day was a grand occasion.

A train sheet for Streetsville Station, the Junction Station, dated September 19, 1879, gives a list of Conductors, Engineers, Firemen, etc., this record preserved because it referred to the Special Train taking the Governor General to Milton and returning for the official opening of the railway. On the run from Toronto to Milton, the Conductor was Flanagan, the Engineer was Spragge and the Fireman was Phipps. Even the baggageman, Ryan, on this particular run is listed. On the return trip, the Special carried the same conductor and baggageman but changed Engineer and Fireman to Greenshields and Cameron respectively. The train left Toronto at 10:55 a.m., cleared Streetsville Junction at 11:25 and arrived at Milton at 11:46 a.m. On the return trip the record indicates a departure from Milton at 12:26 through Streetsville Junction at 12:51, Lambton at 1:12 and arriving in Toronto at 1:35 p.m. From this schedule it is quite evident that the official opening ceremonies were brief, since the Marquis of Lorne spent less than an hour at Milton, including having his picture taken in the midst of the official group.

In his book, *The Trail of the Swinging Lantern,* John M. Copeland details a photograph of the official party standing before a banner which reads, 'Success to the C.V.R....Welcome to Lorne'. Among those identified was George Laidlaw, the promoter and president of the line. Others in the photograph were John C. Bailey, the engineer of the C.V.R. and Harry Crew, his assistant. Many prominent personages accompanied the Governor General, among them the Honourable George W. Allan, Senator;

the Honourable John McMurrich, M.L.C., Toronto; James Beatty, K.C., Mayor of Toronto; Wm. Taylor, secretary for James Ross, the young Scottish surveyor and engineer in charge of construction, and Ross McKenzie, accountant with the C.V.R. who later became one of Canada's most famous lacrosse players.

The entry of a railway into the town that helped to sponsor it was usually a gala affair. Write-ups of the opening of the railway and the first sod-turning at Milton indicate that a good crowd of people attended, numbering several hundred and including the Governor General. Not so at Orangeville when the C.V.R. finally arrived on December 4, 1879. "The first engine crossed Broadway on Monday evening at 5 p.m.", states the Orangeville "Sun", "the men on the mainline had been hard at work for sometime previously. By 4 p.m. on Monday, the rails were laid as far as the station and soon after the iron horse came steaming along with several flat cars of rails attached. Quite a crowd of citizens were present on this auspicious occasion. A temporary platform was erected below the station where the hard-worked and exhausted men were treated to refreshments. The C.V.R. employees' thanks for the kindly manner in which they were treated at the conclusion of the road were due not, we are ashamed to confess, to the town of Orangeville but to an ordinary citizen Mr. H. Haley."

Less than a week later on December 11, 1879 the same paper headlines an article "A reduction wanted!", saying "Now that the C.V.R. is in running order people are expecting a reduction in the fare to Toronto. It is one of the advantages we looked for on completion of the road. Return tickets should be issued between the different points on the line. At present neither on the C.V.R. or the T.G. & B. Railway are return tickets to be had. The policy pursued by the latter road hitherto seems to have been to make as much money as possible. The convenience of the public was little considered. Return tickets to Toronto ought to be had for $2.00, and if the C.V.R. makes a move at once in the matter, the public will not be slow to appreciate its action." The idea was coolly received by the Laidlaw interests and never acted upon by the railway.

Even before the formal opening of the railway in 1879, regular trains were running between Milton and Parkdale, with a bus service from Parkdale to the Toronto Union Station carrying about six hundred passengers per day to and from the Toronto Exhibition.

The Milton "Canadian Champion" files contain the diary of a Mr. David Downey, an employee of the McCallum Quarries at Milton. From a small entry therein we learn that the first train into Milton arrived on December 7, 1876. Since the official opening was September 19, 1879, some three years later, we can only assume that it was a construction train, and, however, that the railway was progressing rapidly but not without difficulty.

Mrs. C.T. Gerrie, in her history of Belwood, mentions that "the first train came into Belwood Station on November 18, 1879 and was a great day for rejoicing. The school was let out for the day and all the children were permitted to have a ride on the train. It then backed up about a mile, with the children on board and came into the station again. A few farmers were quite upset as they had not been paid for their land which was taken and even put rail fences across the tracks. However this trouble was soon settled when they got their money." Mr. Gerrie, in a letter to the author recalls his father speaking of this story, since he himself was one of the children who received the free ride.

Cooksville Station, C.V.R. - 1884; *Mrs. M. Belleghem photo*

RIDING THE TRAIN

To experience the days of the early railway it is necessary to "ride the train". With a little imagination, we will now travel by the Credit Valley Railway from Toronto to Orangeville, making a trip from one terminus to another over the toughest terrain that the railway encountered.

We begin as our engine arrives at the Toronto Union Station located in the centre of this thriving metropolis. She is the "J.L. Morrison", Engine #19 built at Kingston, Ontario in 1882. Her type is a 4-4-0 with 69" drivers and 16x24" cylinders. Slowly she moves on to our waiting train as black smoke belches from her stack. Our train consists of two head-end baggage-box cars and four coaches, since this is Monday and passenger traffic is brisk and the local freight shipments are heavy. The scene at the station is one of hustle and bustle as friends and passengers make farewells and businessmen load their wares onto baggage cars. There are no porters and everyone carries his or her own hand baggage. Immigrants, headed for the deep back-country now that almost all of central and southern Ontario has been settled, stand beside their total belongings, awaiting the word of the stationmaster to load; their worldly possessions seem so meagre and the open doors of the baggage-box cars look like gaping mouths waiting to gobble up everything on the platform at the stationmaster's signal.

Grunting and clanking like some fierce bull, our engine waits. Suddenly a piercing shriek of the whistle announces the completion of loading-boarding preparations, and we slowly move out of the arched sheds of the old Union Station on the trackage of the Grand Trunk Railway and into the blazing sunshine. A six foot high board fence partially blocks our view to the south, a symbol of the rivalry with the Northern Railway, a blatant physical barrier erected to separate the trackages.

As we clank and bump slowly over the trackage of our competitors we see the Ontario Government Parliament Buildings on our right. This edifice is the largest building in Toronto and dominates the young city skyline. Situated between Simcoe and John Sts., it faces Front St. West and backs onto Wellington St., occupying almost a complete city block.

To our left is the vast expanse of the Grand Trunk passenger and freight yard, with the Toronto Harbour background. Through the pall of smoke which hangs over this area due to the many switch engines bustling back and forth, we can look across this vast array of cars and trackage and see, at the water's edge, the focus of all the legal problems described earlier: here is the Credit Valley freight shed, its four-track storage yard and the single-track spur which leads out onto the Credit Valley wharf.

We grind past the Toronto Waterworks at the foot of John St., past the Grand Trunk Elevators at Peter St. and under the Brock St. footbridge (Spadina Avenue), and slowly past another railway in Toronto, the yards and engine facilities of the Northern Railway. This yard extends from Brock St. to the Queens Wharf at the foot of Bathurst Street. Just beyond the Northern yards we can see the passenger and freight terminal facilities of Toronto, Grey and Bruce Railway at the foot of Bathurst Street directly south of Old Fort York.

Between Bathurst St. and Tecumseh St. we slowly cross the mainlines of the Grand Trunk and the Northern Railways, the two major railways in Ontario, and ease onto the right-of-way and trackage of the Credit Valley Railway. On our right we see the sheds of the Western Cattle Market and to the left the engine facilities of the Toronto, Grey and Bruce. Next stop is Parkdale, and from our apparent increase in speed, it is easy to see that our engine crew are on home ground and know the speed that our right-of-way will allow. We pass the industrial complexes of the Massey Manufacturing Company and Dominion Bridge Company to the north while the Central Prison passes by on the lakeside to our left. We cross King St., notice the Provincial Lunatic Asylum sandwiched between King and Queen Sts., its high wall, dome towers and greyish buildings reminiscent of some debtors prison of old.

After crossing King St., we approach the Parkdale Station set to the southwest of the Credit Valley trackage. Here are the main terminal facilities of the Credit Valley Railway with its many freight and passenger sidings, its roundhouse, turntable and repair depot. These are located in the general area of King and Dufferin Sts., in the northeast corner extending north from King St. up to Queen, parallel to Dufferin St. At Parkdale our tender is loaded with coal, for this is the last point from which we are able to obtain coal until our return. From here on we will burn wood, and at most of the stations, the wood will be piled and waiting to be loaded while the passengers and station agents handle inbound and outbound freight.

After a lengthy stop at Parkdale, we move out, at an only slightly accelerated speed, toward the Junction. When we crossed Dufferin St. at Queen St. we left the actual city of Toronto behind, for Dufferin St. was the west city boundary, and it is evident by the large sections of open land that we are now in the "suburbs". It is easy to predict that some day soon all this open land will be overtaken by development and that the city will devour the hamlet called the Junction, which is just ahead, and probably continue beyond. We approach the Junction slowly and one can see that this is a significant junction of railways and will someday be a major railway terminal. Here the lines of the Grand Trunk, the Toronto, Grey and Bruce, and the Credit Valley pass, cross, or merge with one another for interchange. Here someday will be facilities for expansion of railway freight handling as yet undreamed.

It is easy to look back and predict the future; even the prediction is 'ancient history' now. As we can see by a map of the Junction, by 1866 the trackage became quite complicated and, indeed, the Junction was a railway hub for many years. Not until the advent of the diesel locomotive and the tremendous expansion of the city of Toronto well beyond the Junction did the importance of this centre begin to recede. Even today the Junction remains a major station for passenger trains on the C.P.R. and a complex yard facility for local industry and freight car handling.

Our train of 1882 steams slowly into the Junction; the station scene resembles those at Union Station and Parkdale, and similar scenes will be at every station on the trip all the way to Orangeville; the arrival of the train in the depot will activate a bustle of fond farewells, joyous hellos, embarking and disembarking businessmen, local tradespeople loading, stacking goods for shipment, picking up raw materials. Modern efficient methods for transport of rail shipments onto railway-owned trucks for direct delivery exclude this aspect of trade essential to the merchant of 1882. The railway station was a hub of activity and an area of interchange of news and information that is nowhere duplicated today.

Leaving the Junction, we head westward, across the open fields of farmlands near Summerville, toward our next stop, Lambton Mills. (The station here is situated west of the intersection of what is now Jane St. and St. Clair Ave. West.) Our stop is brief, and we once again plod westward crossing the Humber River near the village of Summerville. (To locate this accurately for the reader today, the area is very near the immense interchange of Highways #5 and 27) Our train rattles across the trestle over the river and open land into Dixie Station. The population of Dixie at this date is about 150; the village consists of two carpenter shops, a blacksmith shop, three churches, a large brick schoolhouse and a hotel. The general store does an extensive business and the hotel is well patronized; no large industries or mills provide freight, however, and so our stop is primarily for passengers returning home after a trip to the "big city".

Soon we arrive at Cooksville, with its population of 300. Prior to the disastrous fire of 1852, it was a lively little village with all kinds of businesses flourishing and now, in 1882, with the coming of the Credit Valley, some of the business is beginning to return. Here gas-oil is being loaded onto the train for delivery to the famous Barber Brothers factory at Streetsville. Gas-oil (gasoline) is a local product of the refinery of Parker and Gordon of Cooksville, which, coupled with the products of a carriage factory and a steam saw mill, provide additional freight. Our stop at this station is of considerable length. Cooksville is the home of the Canadian Vine Growers Association whose farm of thirty acres provides grapes which produce 50,000 gallons of wine per year.

Streetsville Station, C.V.R. - as it is to-day; *Author's photo*

Moving slowly out of Cooksville, we head in a more northerly direction now, into the back country towards Streetsville. Here are extensive railway facilities to enable us to meet inbound trains from St. Thomas and to pass each other in safety. Streetsville is the junction of the Credit Valley mainline to St. Thomas and the branch to Orangeville. This is the site of the famous C.V.R. wye; enabling the turning of complete trains as well as allowing movements from St. Thomas to Orangeville, Orangeville to Toronto or St. Thomas to Toronto. Streetsville is the home of the Barber Brothers, world famous woollen producers, and the home of the large grist mills of

Gooderham and Worts. Here too are the mills of R.R. Beatty and the hosiery factory of Issac Staton. It is a bustling, energetic town with a population in excess of 675 persons. After much freight is unloaded and loaded, the track switches are lined up and our locomotive leads us across a network of rails and slowly begins the northward trip over gently rising land towards Brampton.

Brampton, the seat of the County Government of the County of Peel, has a population in excess of 2000. Brampton became a town in 1873 and is a first class grain market. The town has three schools, two banks, two telegraph offices, five hotels, four doctors, eight lawyers and many factories. One of these the Haggart Brothers factory, a four-storey building on Main St. devoted to the manufacturing of threshing machines and stoves is clearly visible as we enter Brampton. Also visible are huge lumber piles for the Haggart works; the yard covers two acres of land and the raw materials provide a large amount of freight traffic for the railway. In Brampton our tracks cross those of the Grand Trunk and, after a long station stop, we are on our way, crossing the diamond trackage of the Grand Trunk and climbing slowly away from the town and upward toward the Caledon Hills.

The next stop is Cheltenham, another of the many waterfed mill towns that mark the route of the Credit Valley as it winds its way northward. The station lies about one-half mile east of the town, and, because the town is situated in a valley on the Credit River, we can see just the odd trace of smoke rising amongst the trees. Our conductor tells us that the population is about three hundred and the town is very prosperous, with many mills, a good carriage and wagon factory, two fine hotels and many shops and stores.

Cheltenham Station, C.V.R. - as it was in 1900; *Ralph Beaumont photo*

After a brief stop we begin again, our ever winding climb and shortly pass the settlement of Boston Mills, where we can see the huge three and a half storey frame mill of C.D. Spalding. This mill was originally built in 1860 by Henry Castor and is capable of producing 30,000 pounds of grist and flour annually.

Inglewood Station, C.V.R. and Hamilton and Northwestern Railway - as it was in 1910; *Edgar Ireland photo*

Shortly after Boston Mills we ease our way across the track of the Hamilton and Northwestern Railway. This is Sligo (later to be called Riverdale and as we know it today, Inglewood), a railway junction and nothing more. Our right-of-way seems to have been carved out of the bush like some giant finger pulled through the mass of trees and shrubs and then smoothed. Our train twists and squirms as we continue to climb and enter the glen area of the Caledon Hills. Ahead is some of the most spectacular scenery in Ontario. The triumph of pioneer railroad engineering is evident on every side as we scramble and claw on our narrow ledge, climbing until we can see ahead that the glen has divided and we approach the huge trestle across the Credit River below.

The trestle is an engineering masterpiece in itself, being over 1100 feet in length and 85 feet high. All the discomforts of travelling are quickly forgotten as we gaze out ahead of us up the valley, with our right-of-way and track winding off towards the horizon. To our left as we cross the trestle is

67

Credit Valley Railway Trestle - 1884; *Public Archives of Ontario photo*

the glen leading to Belfountain, and on our right and almost directly below is the settlement of Brimstone. We slow slightly as we cross the trestle and pull past the Forks of Credit station and its siding, with the flat cars loaded with "Brownstone", destined for pickup by the next southbound train and scheduled for the Toronto building trade market. The beautiful scenery continues all the way up the valley to Alton.

Forks of Credit Station, C.V.R. - 1884; *Public Archives of Ontario photo*

Approaching another depot we start to slow again. On our left appears another track slightly above us and soon this line reaches our level and we merge. We have arrived at Cataract, population 300. For the traveller leaving the train at this station, with its array of sidings, engine stall and turntable, the scene is all 'railway' until one looks out over the valley. The view is breathtaking. Directly below the station is the Credit River and less than half a mile south is the Credit Falls, the site of Church's Mill. Somewhere in the vicinity is supposed to be a salt spring which once gave rise to a thought by a certain Mr. Grant to utilize the spring as a source for salt, however none was ever found or produced.

Cataract lays claim to the Credit Valley Gold Rush, begun in 1818 by a rumour that "gold" had been found there. People quit their jobs and began to roam the hillsides. Like the salt, no gold was ever found, and had it not been a railway junction, Cataract would probably exist only as a memory today. As we limber our legs by disembarking from our coach for a few minutes, we note that the town contains a brewery, a large flour mill, general store, post office, woollen factory, saw mill and two hotels. Both village and railway junction have remarkably been carved out of the side of the escarpment, marks of the engineering and drive of the pioneers of Canada.

After taking on water and wood, we start once more on the upward climb towards Alton. The terrain from Cataract to Alton is less severe than the previous ten miles, and the rugged valley of the Credit River begins to level out and emerge as a series of undulating hills rather than a steep-sided gorge. Alton is situated in one of the valleys between these gentle hills and is about a mile and a half from the widely famed Shaw's lake, the major source of the Credit River, and a very famous locaton for bird hunters. Alton is already one of the smartest looking villages of its size in the County of Peel, with a post office, three churches, a beautiful schoolhouse, five general stores, a tin shop,harness shop, shoe store, blacksmith, wagon shop, three grist mills, a flour mill, saw mill and furniture factory, together with two hotels and a large foundry for farm equipment. Nearby are two very large patent lime kilns, large enough to warrant special rail sidings for the transport of the finished products to the large construction trade in Toronto. Indeed, as we slow to our stop at Alton station, we sense the activity of a thriving community and so the importance of the daily trains to and from the metropolitan centres to the south. The train is the vital link with the great world of business, and the station at each of its stops is the axis of the town. Here, and only here, is the news first hand. How is the City?...the Country?...the markets? All these and many more questions vital to everyday living are answered at the depot at train time.

Once again we are jostled, as our engineer does his best, with the light motive power available, to bring our train back to life and to the seemingly never ending climb towards Orangeville.

Soon we rise out of the valley and approach the relatively level run to Orangeville. Farm land has been cleared on either side of our right-of-way; farm outbuildings appear on the horizon as meagre holdings are made more secure; hints of civilization appear. Down the line, we begin to slow again because we are approaching the level crossing with the tracks of the Toronto, Grey and Bruce Railway at Melville Junction. Here we cross the line of another of the Laidlaw promoted railways, ease through the diamond and resume our run north. (Melville, a small hamlet at this time, will eventually almost completely disappear when the water-powered mills give way to steam and the Credit Valley Railway no longer exists.)

As we go through Melville on our train of the 1880's we see another type of back-country gathering place with local mill and general store. Some five hundred yards beyond the village we approach the smallest trestle on the north branch of the C.V.R. and glide, once more, over the Credit River, barely twenty feet above the flood level. The trestle is one hundred and forty-six feet long with short spans of sixteen feet. From here to Orangeville is "smooth sailing" with little grade and fairly uninteresting scenery.

Suddenly we can see ahead the settled town of Orangeville and the end of our journey. Here is the northern terminus of the Credit Valley Railway...freight sheds, sidings, water-tower, coaling facilities, a turntable, repair depot and assorted railway buildings, together with a multi-tracked terminal for passengers. Once more the sights and sounds of the station stops enroute are repeated; this time there are no farewells; this is the end of the line, and glad greetings are offered as friend meets friend with hearty handshake and fond embrace; the businessman unloads his wares; local merchants hopefully look for much needed shipments of supplies. The railway crew uncouple the old style link-and-pin couplers, the engine to be watered and refueled. No return trip will be made until tomorrow; in 1882 one or two trains daily are scheduled.

While we have been struggling from Cataract to Orangeville, one of our counterparts has been running westward with some of our original cars and passengers, destined for Erin, Hillsburg, Garafraxa, Fergus and Elora.

Hillsburg Station, C.V.R. - 1884; *Mrs. William Russell photo*

Fergus Station, C.V.R. - 1880; *Public Archives of Ontario photo*

We would encounter nothing significantly different from the stops made between Toronto and Cataract, except that at Garafraxa we might notice we had left the Credit River watershed and entered the Grand River watershed. The line of watershed is remarkably noticeable on the curve, a rather sharp bend just before our arrival at Garafraxa station (now known as Belwoods). From here to Fergus we would follow the Grand River, first on one side, the east bank, and then crossing over to the west side before we encounter the Elora Gorge and the town of Fergus and its historic mills. Fergus does give us an interchange with the Wellington, Grey and Bruce Railway and sometimes the traffic which originates from here is very brisk. South of Fergus we would continue to Elora, the other terminal of the north branch of the C.V.R. Turntable, engine sheds, station, freight platforms, and the smaller outbuildings all signify that this is another end of the line for the C.V.R.

It is easy today to look at eighty-foot streamlined passenger cars and forget the open vestibule, thirty-eight foot long, hard-seated coach of the C.V.R., yet the papers of the day exclaimed how elegant they were! Nor can **we imagine short, twenty-five foot long freight cars, arch bar trucks, truss** rod underframes and hand brakes, particularly as we look at today's sixty-to-eighty-foot insulated, roller bearing, steel cars with fail-safe air brakes. All the horsepower of the average small railway of the 1870-1880 era is the equivalent of just one diesel locomotive on the average Canadian railway of today.

Chair Car of the 1880's;- *Toronto Public Library photo*

Parlour Car of the 1880's;- *Toronto Public Library photo*

CARS AND TRACK

Canadian Pacific Railway Engine (formerly C.V.R.) 1900; *Mrs. William Russell photo*

In the December 31, 1879 Annual Report of the C.V.R., it was noted that the company now "owns 9 engines and 100 cars and is expected to add in March 1880 an additional 6 engines, 350 freight cars and 18 passenger cars...In the meantime, the company will lease all rolling stock required." Reference to the volume of traffic is found in the Brampton "Conservator", April 9, 1880: "since the new passenger coaches and box cars have been placed upon the road, the passenger and freight traffic has increased very much; sometimes seats in the coaches are not available and the sterner sex must take the smoking car." An article on May 21, 1880 says "They (the C.V.R.) are lately put on some new passenger coaches, which for beauty and elegance compare favourably with any other road."

The cost of equipment is hard to ascertain; the only direct reference to equipment is contained in a short paragraph by Miles Pennington in his book *Railways and Other Ways* (1894). He states that the cost of a box car was about $900 and its average life about eight years. With the ornate design of passenger cars of the 80's, it is extremely difficult to come up with an accurate cost. However, in 'Scientific American' of 1876, the average American passenger car is said to have cost $4423.13.

By October 1, 1880, a through train was running from Orangeville direct to Toronto and was aptly named 'the Orangeville Express', making the trip in under three hours. The Brampton "Conservator" detailed the effectiveness of the railroad on that date, and on November 11, 1881, says "In the meantime the Business of the road is constantly increasing and taxing the carrying capacity to the utmost. New cars are being added to the rolling stock at the rate of from fifteen to twenty per week but the employment could be found for fully four hundred more."

In the official company statement of December 31, 1879, Shanley gave a lengthy report on the trackage of the entire line, including the branches. He said that radius of curvature on the main line was 1910 feet with a ratio of straight track to curved track of 9 to 16 over 96 miles. On the branches the radius of curvature was 850 feet with a ratio of straight to curve of two to three over 35 miles on the Orangeville Branch and over 27 miles on the Elora Branch.

Steepest gradients on the mainline have an inclination of one in 100 or 53 feet to the mile. On the branches the maximum gradient is one in 130 feet or 70 feet to the mile.

Rail, as reported by Shanley, is 56 pound per yard for all trackage.

None of this rail has been found by the author during his research and so it is safe to say that all had been replaced by the C.P.R. after the 1884 takeover. Rail at Cataract leading to the spur (originally the lead track to the old turntable) is dated 1890 and is the oldest found on this particular section of the railway.

The company, in attempting to promote passenger traffic, utilized the beauty of the countryside adjacent to the railway and in 1880 the Brampton "Conservator" of April 9 reports that "During the past few days C.J. Wheelock and a staff of engineers has been engaged in laying out a park and a pleasure grounds between the falls (Church's Falls) and the Forks which will embrace some very fine scenery said to excel the White Mountains of Vermont or any in Canada. Tourists will be much gratified with the view of the Forks, Forks Bridge, Picture Rocks, Devil's Pulpit and the Falls. We strongly urge Sunday Schools and others planning excursions to patronize the Credit Valley and see the finest scenery in Canada, unexcelled by anything on the American Continent. We are informed that the railway company will offer very liberal rates to the new park." It is noteworthy that Laidlaw was able to plan a park in 1880 that encompassed all the area presently being developed, almost one hundred years later, by the Ontario Government as a Provincial Park, opening up the area once again for tourists to enjoy the same beautiful countryside and local landmarks dormant such a long time. It is indeed a shame that the area cannot be served by a train rather than automobiles.

The railways of the day were always trying to attract passengers in one way or another, local papers advertising 'up and coming' excursions to local parks for picnics or parties. Typical of these is an advertisement from the July 27, 1883 Brampton 'Conservator' under the heading "Excursion on Civic Holiday, August 8": "An excursion to Niagara Falls and return will be given under the auspices of the P.M. church choir of Brampton. A special train both ways on the Credit Valley Railway and a steamer from Toronto. The special train will leave Brampton Station at 6 a.m. returning at 9 p.m. giving six hours to view the beauties of Niagara Falls and surrounding attractions. The train will run alongside the steamer at Brock St. thus eliminating all dangers and delays crossing the tracks, etc. Tickets for the round trip only $1.50, children under twelve 75¢." The C.V.R. was anxious to promote passenger traffic, local traffic to other areas as well as Toronto traffic to the country. The excursion train was always popular, even up until the late thirties, when the use of the automobile forecast the downfall of the passenger train. The C.P.R., having taken over from the Credit Valley, continued to sponsor excursions; records indicate that excursion trains into the area served by the Credit Valley, were being run as late as 1945. One of the highlights of the C.P.R. era was the Company picnic held at Fairy Lake in Erin, with special excursion trains bringing employees and their families from all over the division.

Alfred Price, in *Credit Valley Memoirs,* tells of two antiquated parlour cars being bought from the New York Central and placed on the run from St. Thomas to Toronto. The rear ends of the cars were rounded and painted and renamed 'Victoria' and 'Humber'. No record is available to indicate to what trains these cars were attached, but it can be imagined that they would constitute the ultimate in travel advantages for the newly-founded C.V.R.

The following is the Credit Valley Locomotive Roster as recorded at the time of the take-over by the Canadian Pacific Railway, 1884.

C.V.R. No.	C.P.R. No.	Type	Driv. Wheel	Cylinder Size	Builder	Bldr. No.	Year	Addenda
1	178	4-4-0	69	17x24	Portland	296	1874	RE#1905-103 1912-7016 1913-Scrap
2	179	4-4-0	69	17x24	Portland	298	1874	Re#1905-104 Scrap-1911
3	191	4-4-0	62	17x24	Brooke		1873	Re#1905-16 Scrap-1909
4	192	4-4-0	62	17x24	Brooke		1873	Sold 1903
5	193	4-4-0	62	17x24	Brooke		1873	Re#1905-17 Scrap-1910
6	195	4-4-0	63	15x24	Origin Unknown			Scrap-1888
8	180	4-4-0	62	17x24	Kingston	199	1879	Scrap-1897
12	189	4-4-0	69	16x24	Manchester	836	1880	Scrap-1899
13	190	4-4-0	69	16x24	Manchester	837	1880	Scrap-1899
14	181	4-4-0	62	17x24	Kingston	237	1881	Scrap-1897
15	182	4-4-0	62	17x24	Kingston	220	1881	Scrap-1897
16	183	4-4-0	62	17x24	Kingston	225	1882	Scrap-1899
17	184	4-4-0	62	17x24	Kingston	226	1882	Re#1905-43 Scrap-1909
18	185	4-4-0	69	16x24	Kingston	233	1882	Scrap-1896
19	186	4-4-0	69	16x24	Kingston	234	1882	Re#1905-13 Scrap-1908
20	187	4-4-0	69	16x24	Kingston	235	1882	Re#1905-14 Scrap-1910
21	188	4-4-0	69	16x24	Kingston	236	1882	Re#1905-15 Scrap-1910
266	194	4-4-0	63	16x21	Origin Unknown			Scrap-1898
584	196	4-4-0	50	16x24	Danforth			Scrap-1888
30					Possibly N&NW loco or H&NW loco Reference to use on construction trains....Brampton "Conservator"			

It is interesting to note that locomotive #1 of the C.V.R. was the last engine to be scrapped by the C.P.R. in 1913.

RAILWAY PEOPLE

In 1880 five men worked together on the Credit Valley Railway. They were all young men getting their start in life. They worked hard and well, and the railway that they built became an important factor in developing the City of Toronto and the Province of Ontario.

The names of the five men were: James Ross, William Mackenzie, Herbert Holt, George D. Perry and H.E. Suckling. Perry was a clerk in one of the railway's offices; Ross was starting as superintendent of the line; Mackenzie received various small contracts such as stations and worksheds; Suckling was Secretary-Treasurer of the company; and Holt, the young Irishman from Dublin, was a graduate civil engineer, and assumed the duties as the railway's engineer. All of these young men were fast, firm friends.

Each one of these men made his mark in Canada, and each became a leader in his own field. Three of them joined forces after the Credit Valley Railway was completed and, together with another young man named Donald Mann, they formed the contracting firm of Ross, Holt, Mackenzie and Mann, building many of the prairie and mountain sections of the Canadian Pacific Railway. Holt later became Chief Engineer of the C.P.R. prairie and mountain sections until its completion at Craigellachie. He then returned to Montreal, formed a syndicate which combined the Montreal Gas Company and the Royal Electric Company and which eventually grew to the gigantic Montreal Light, Heat and Power Consolidation, one of the most amazingly successful public utility corporations in the world. He also built dams and power distribution systems elsewhere in Canada, became interested in the Royal Bank and eventually helped it to become the second largest bank in Canada.

Perry, never the dreamer but rather the hard, steady worker, accomplished, by working up through the ranks, the position as General Manager of the Great Northwestern Telegraph Company, although he had never learned to operate a telegraph key.

James Ross rehabilitated the street railways of Toronto and Montreal, after having remained for many years previously in the railway building field. He also acquired interests in some big British Utility Companies and, when he died, left one of the largest fortunes ever accumulated in Canada.

H.E. Suckling came to Montreal about the time that the others left the Credit Valley line, and staying with the C.P.R., he eventually worked his way up to become the Treasurer of the huge corporation.

William Mackenzie became one of the greatest of "Canadian Builders". His imagination and power of personality, his vision and his determination eventually gave birth and helped to successfully achieve Canada's second great transcontinental railway. It is said that because of the type of man he was, when he died, none were too poor or too rich to pay him tribute. Such were the men that George Laidlaw chose to help him to establish the Credit Valley Railway.

No story of the Credit Valley Railway could be complete without the background of the people who envisioned it and of those who built it and ran it. One family connected with the building of the C.V.R. was the McEnaney's of Cataract. Patrick McEnaney Sr. came originally from Ireland, settling in the village of Silvercreek, Caledon Township. With the coming of the C.V.R., the family moved to Cataract. Patrick was born in 1826 and died in 1897; his wife Ann was born in 1836 and died in 1903. They had ten children, six boys and four girls. The eldest son, Peter, was engaged for many years as a construction foreman on the C.V.R. Born in 1854, he never married but made his home in Cataract. According to old timers he used to boast that he was one of the first persons to own a regulation railway watch. Tradition also says that he could get more work out of a construction gang than any other man on the railway. He died in 1938 at the age of 84.

The next McEnaney to enter the employ of the C.V.R. was Patrick Jr. He operated a steam shovel loading construction cars with gravel from the company-owned pits. Born in 1860, he was the musician of the family and played the violin. Many stories are told of his entertaining his fellow workers after hours in the railway boarding cars. He lived at Cataract, never married, and died in 1927 at the age of 67. Although the remaining four sons also worked for the railway, their employer was not the Credit Valley Railway but rather its successor, the C.P.R. Dougal, born in 1868, started as a trainman with the C.P.R. eventually becoming a conductor on the run between Toronto and Hamilton. He died in 1940 at the age of 72. Archibald (1873-1944) and Joseph (1870-1950) also became railway employees and both also became conductors.

Though not directly employed by the C.V.R., Frank (Francis) McEnaney, born in 1856, operated the Junction House Hotel, adjacent to the Cataract Station. Stories are told of the rollicking parties given for

THE SECOND AND THIRD GENERATION IN CANADA.

THE CATARACT McENANEYS

1889

| Mary Ann | Peter | Patrick J. | Francis | Dougal Thomas |
| 1863-1936 | 1854-1938 | 1860-1927 | 1856-1922 | 1868-1940 |

| Katherine | Patrick (Sr.) | Ann | Elizabeth |
| 1865-1917 | 1826-1897 | 1836-1908 | 1867-1952 |

| Archibald | Alice | J. Joseph |
| 1873-1944 | 1875-1960 | 1870-1950 |

Vincent X. McEnaney photo

Junction House Hotel, Cataract, 1884; *Vincent X. McEnaney photo*

selected persons when the music of brother Patrick could be heard through the valley. The evening would grow late, the parties ranged on and many a guest at the party ended up a guest of the hotel for the night, or until at least sun-up when he was able to find his way home. When the liquor licenses of the five hotels in Caledon Township were revoked in 1907 and prohibition settled in, Frank gave up the hotel business and moved to Toronto. A blacksmith by trade, he teamed up with his son, Gordon, doing construction work for the Canadian Pacific Railway on its Guelph to Goderich line. Francis died in 1922 at the age of 68; Gordon died of a heart attack while on the job.

Elizabeth (1867-1952), in a way upholding the railway tradition of the family, became the wife of a C.P.R. conductor.

Delving into many local histories which have been published and reading many unpublished manuscripts relating to the Credit Valley Railway, has never uncovered a family so involved in railroading as the McEnaneys. In a history such as this, credit must be given to the pioneers, for they built it, lived with it, and, eventually, made it run. Unfortunately, little is recorded about these people, and so it remains that their efforts can only be acknowledged in minor ways.

Mr. John Howard was the first agent at Cataract Station, followed by

82

Thomas Sanderson, James Phillips and Fred Wilson of Alton. Phillips retired in 1932, while Wilson became the last agent and closed the station when passenger traffic was taken off the line in 1958.

George Herbert was the first agent at Forks of the Credit Station and after twenty-five years as agent, was found dead at the station in 1907. Mr. Riddell was the first agent at Alton and J.D. Leitch had that honour at Erin.

In 1887, the Brampton "Conservator" reported the appointment of Thomas Bowles, Reeve of Chinguacousy Township as a County Director of the C.V.R. while the same paper reports that Mr. Lovelock was made a Conductor on the Express train from Orangeville to Toronto. This item, dated Friday December 12, 1879, also stated that he was the conductor for some time previous on construction trains. In the time sheet giving information on the Marquis of Lorne Special through Streetsville Junction, there is a Lovelock listed as a conductor on a ballast train #341 with Kean, Webster, and McGillis as engineer, fireman and brakeman respectively. Both of these trains are listed as Eastbound and as having come off the Orangeville Branch.

In the Perkins Bull Historical Series, "From Macdonnell to McGuigan", reference is made to John Markle, "a clever mechanic, he started in business as a builder and shortly became the Credit Valley Railway Company's bridge engineer".

The Woodstock "Sentinel" of October 2, 1874 details a tour of inspection starting from Toronto, and relates that the tour saw the work of the railways' own forces, since the route north from Streetsville was constructed entirely by the railway's own men. An average of 600 to 700 men were employed according to the article under the direction of J.C. Bailey, chief engineer; John McColman, resident engineer on the mainline; D. McKenzie, resident engineer on the Peel and Wellington branch; Mr. Brothers and E.A. Walsh, officials under Mr. McColman and Mr. Thomas Watts, superintendent of bridges.

The first timetable book used at Hillsburgh Station is dated January 20, 1880 and the agent was W.A. Munroe. Other agents were Peter Ward, George Walker, William Little, Jim Russell and Ed Griner. Hillsburgh Station and grain elevator, burned in the fall of 1932, were replaced with a small station in 1933.

MEMORABILIA

Primitive Painting by "Chief Beaver" 1884 - showing Junction House Hotel and Cataract Station; *Vincent X. McEnaney photo*

There is a tremendous amount of miscellaneous data and facts which appear during the research for any writing, which should be noted. In 1869 railways ran according to local time; the International Railway and Steam Navigation Guide of July 1869 indicates that trains running from Montreal to Toronto were on Montreal time, Toronto to Sarnia on Toronto time, Toronto to Buffalo on Toronto time, but arrivals in Buffalo are shown in New York time. The confusion which must have arisen in transcontinental timetables must have been immense. Not only were the gauges of the railways different but the time varied with the railway and even within cities on the same road. It was not until November 26, 1883 that all Canadian railways except the Michigan Central adopted the twenty-four hour clock system. According to the Railroad Magazine of April 1972, the railroads adopted Standard Time on November 18, 1883, but the new time did not become official until the U.S. Congress passed the Standard Time Act on March 19, 1918. With this new system some semblance of order came into railway timetables.

Credit Valley Railway

Running in Connection with Port Dover Railway.

NO. 2   **TIME TABLE,**   **NO. 2,**

Taking effect Monday, 9th September, 1878.

Miles.	GOING EAST.		STATIONS.		GOING WEST.		Miles.
	No.1.	No.3.			No.2.	No.4.	
	A.M.	P.M.			A.M.	P.M.	
0	7.40	4.00	Dep.	Ingersoll. Arr.	9.15	5.25	10
2	7.45	4.05		× Centreville.	9.10	5.20	8
5	7.55	4.15		Beachville.	9.00	5.10	5
10	8.10	4.30		Woodstock.	8.45	4.55	0
—	8.15	4.35	Arr.	Woodstock, P.D.&L.H.R'y. Dep.	8.40	4.50	—

× Flag Station—Will stop on signal.

C. LAIDLAW,

September, 1878.   **Managing Director.**

C.V.R. Timetable; *Canadian Pacific Railway photo*

Every railway at one time or another has its accident, which unfortunately for those involved, brings the railway into the public eye with dramatic impact: not so the C.V.R.

Laidlaw's narrow-gauge Toronto, Grey and Bruce Railway had its spectacular Horseshoe Curve wreck in the Caledon Mountain area between Cardwell Junction and Caledon (September 3, 1907), but the railway had been under C.P.R. control for 23 years and could hardly be classified as a T.G. & B. accident. Likewise, on the Credit Valley line, the only major accident occurred at the Forks of the Credit trestle long after the C.V.R. had ceased to be under the control of the original owners, and it too was under C.P.R. authority.

Accidents of a more minor nature did occur and the Brampton

"Conservator" of Friday November 28, 1879 relates that "An accident oc-curred on the C.V.R. Monday morning about two miles south of Church's Falls by which a man named Murphy had a collar bone and shoulder blade broken. A gang of sectionmen were coming up the line with a handcar and when in Dolly's Cut, engine #30 overtook them. The sectionmen got their car off the track but there not being room in the cut for the handcar, the men raised it up on its side and while Murphy was holding it, the engine struck it, smashing the handcar and crushing Murphy between it and the bank. He is not seriously hurt and the doctor thinks he will be able to go to his home in Streetsville in a day or two."

The June 10th,1881 edition reports,"A man named McMann was killed at the Forks of the Credit last Friday; he was struck by a car on the new track laid for facilitating the moving of stone from the premises of K. Chisholm and Co. Quarries to the C.V. Railway. He had disobeyed orders of his superintendent for moving the car, by unhooking the cables used to regulate the loaded car down the incline. Mr. McMann and some others were stan-ding on the bridge down below when the car came with lightning speed and all but McMann got out of the way."

The mainline of the railway had its problems too, for at Milton on June 17, 1881 "a serious accident occurred this AM on the C.V.R. ballast train. When nearing the station, a broken wheel on one of the ballast cars caused the car to be thrown from the track, killing one man and injuring several others; one having his collarbone broken, one a broken arm, one bruised about the hips. Those on the last car escaped injury."

The "Canadian Champion" of Milton, Ontario for September 8, 1881 reports a fatal accident: "While the sectionmen on the C.V. line here were coming down the road on a jigger about the 1st line Trafalgar on Tuesday evening, one of their number, Thomas White, fell off in front of the car, and it passed over him, killing him instantly. It is supposed that he was struck on the temple by the driving wheel. White had been in Milton for about four months. He is supposed to have a wife from whom he is divorced."

The foregoing are typical of accidents which plagued the railway. However, the story of a railway would not be complete without some reference to its safety record, and from the evidence available, the Credit Valley Railway faired much better than most of its competitors in this facet of its operations. The one major accident , when one of its promoters was killed has been described fully in a previous chapter. We choose not to classify this as a C.V.R. accident but rather place the blame where the inves-tigating committee assessed it ... directly on the shoulders of the Grand Trunk Railway. It would appear from the lack of accident reports that the C.V.R.,even during construction, was a safe railway to work on and an even safer one to travel on.

An excerpt from the Nassagaweya "Centennial" printed by the Acton Free Press (1950) is entitled "Rail and Bus Service" — "It appears that a rather unusual incident occurred when the Credit Valley went to cross the right-of-way of the old Northwestern railway at Milton. It seems that in those days there were no running rights for any other company to cross a line of a company already established. If any company building a line could get their train across the running line however they could establish their right to continue. As the Northwestern Railway Company had been running from Burlington to Allandale for some years it made it hard for the C.V.R. to get across the other track. When the C.V.R. had their train ready to travel they started out from Toronto and got as far as the Milton Diamond. They could go no further for a while as the Northwestern Company had a train over their tracks. It is said by old timers that after a short conversation by both crews, the crew of the C.V.R. train got off their train and mounted the other train and threw the crew of the Northwestern train off. The C.V.R. crew then took charge and drove the train off the right-of-way. After they accomplished this, they got back on their own train, which was a repair train and had on board all the necessary equipment to finish the rail and were soon over the disputed crossing. Once over, the C.V.R. had their running rights and there was no more trouble." Much research in railway history seems to indicate that this is a standard story for almost every railway.

To the plus side of the ledger of the exploits of the Credit Valley must go the fact that all the "Brownstone" buildings that make up a major portion of the older buildings of Toronto, arrived there by way of the C.V.R. The Chisholm sandstone quarried at the Forks of the Credit and at Inglewood, which was used in building the Ontario Parliament Buildings now standing at the head of University Avenue in Toronto, came out of the back country on the flat cars and gondolas of the C.V.R. Toronto City Hall of Bay Street is another of the well-known "Brownstone" structures.

North of Caledon Lake, near Orangeville, was the shortest railway ever built in Peel County. It was an industrial line used to take marl, used in the manufacture of mortar, from the beds north of the lake to the processing plant at Orangeville, a distance of three miles. There it was processed and shipped on the Credit Valley to supply the building trade in Toronto and many other growing communities throughout Ontario.

In 1909, the C.P.R. built a spur line from the south end of its yard just below the old coal shute, over to the Credit Valley line and followed its roadbed to the old C.V.R. station location, and then on new roadbed proceeded beyond the end of the C.V.R. right-of-way to the Owen Sound Quarries in Mono Township adjacent to the Hockley Road. Stone was brought from this quarry for many years over this spur. The line was finally abandoned when the quarry activity ceased and trackage and ties were then removed.

With additional communications provided by the coming of the C.V.R. — the Grand Trunk Railway having been previously built between 1856 and 1859 — the two railways passed through Brampton, and the village obtained town status, later to become the County Seat. Streetsville, which was a thriving community in the 1850's suffered stagnation until the C.V.R. passed through in 1879. Streetsville complained about the location of its station and by February 1880, the Brampton "Conservator" tells that "it is some satisfaction to find that the C.V.R. Company are erecting another station house at the junction and particularly so to those abiding in the west end; the other station being in the extreme east and surrounded with innumerable quagmires, things that are thought to be rather behind the age." Burnhamthorpe, Palestine, Clairville, Tullamore and Huttonville might have remained thriving communities had the rail line not bypassed them. It is interesting to note that many of the early commuters on the C.V.R. were students who might otherwise not have been able to have access to a secondary education. In the Home Knowledge Atlas of 1888, the following passage indicates that the impact of the railway was felt everywhere it wandered: "Woodstock, which now claims the rank of a city, is a remarkable illustration of what the pluck and enterprise of two or three sagacious residents will do to develope a town. When the Credit Valley Railway was still a paper scheme, laughed at in Parliamentary Committee rooms, and generally much discredited, a few citizens of Woodstock took this 'visionary' scheme in hand, shaped it into a business venture and by sheer pluck and persistence made the new railroad a great highway of commerce. Other railways have since been brought to Woodstock, and with them have come several new industries, so that it would be difficult to set limits to the future achievements of this, the youngest of Ontario cities."

One of the major reasons for the railway's existence was to carry cordwood. So important was this item to the city dweller that the actual papers of incorporation listed the terms of its rates and regulations for its carriage. Item #41 of the articles of Incorporation of the C.V.R. state "The Railway Company shall at all times receive and carry cordwood or any wood or fuel at a rate not to exceed, for dry wood, two and a half cents per mile per cord and from all stations exceeding fifty miles, and at a rate not to exceed three cents per mile from all stations under fifty miles in full car loads; and for green wood at the rate of two and one half cents per ton per mile. The Company shall further, at all times, furnish every facility necessary for the free and unrestrained traffic in cordwood to as large an extent as in the case of other freight carried over said railway." It is known that in 1867, cordwood was selling retail in Toronto at $7.50 to $8.00 per cord. In

Laidlaw's "Reports and Letters on Light Narrow Gauge Railways", printed by Globe Printing of Toronto in 1867, he continually refers to the movement of cordwood and says that "in the City of Toronto there is consumed annually $350,000 worth of cordwood and $200,000 worth of imported coal." Cordwood was big business in the early days of railroading and all four of George Laidlaw's railways were originally intended to handle wood into the Toronto markets. In the case of the C.V.R., the wood issue, although important enough to incorporate into its charter, was not the main reason or concern of the railway in the final analysis. It appears that such was the case in the beginning, but it eventually gave way to the stronger economic pull of through traffic routing from the U.S. via the C.V.R. and Toronto to the seaboard.

A series of reports from the Brampton "Conservator" provide an extremely clear picture of the events which took place from the fall of 1881 until the fall of 1883 and give proof that the statement just made concerning the switch in purpose of the railway is quite true. On November 11, 1881 a report reads "Great prospects for the future prosperity of the C.V.R. The strong opposition which met the C.V.R. to become one of our railways is gradually giving way to a desire to reap its competitive powers and some of its once bitter opponents are endeavouring to secure connections with it. One of the latest converts is the Royal City of Guelph, and a meeting of the Board of Trade there is called to meet next week to consider the advisability of making the necessary arrangements with the road for a branch line. Although the company will endeavour to penetrate every section where a paying business can be done it still has much to attend to before making any purely speculative ventures. A bonus of $65,000 is offered by Elmira for a branch line ten miles long from Elora and next week Mr. Holt will proceed to make the necessary preliminary surveys." The report goes on to say that "its connections with the west and southwest have proved a success and is diverting considerable traffic which hithertofore has gone over the older and better established roads which now must look to their laurels. Work is still being done along the line: new stations have been erected at Hornby, Leslie and Dumfries and two gangs of men have just completed a contract of repairing the Humber Bridge at Lambton Mills. The work on the new freight sheds at Brampton commenced this week, and the foundations have been laid for a new grain elevator and altogether the affairs of the road are in a much more prosperous condition than could have been expected by its most sanguine supporters a year ago."

The picture, as outlined, must have appeared rosy but it is reported that about this time George Laidlaw tried to sell the entire railway for a paltry sum, but he was unable to find any takers.

END OF RAIL

The Brampton "Conservator" of Friday April 9, 1880 reports that "On Monday last, quite a commotion was raised in our village, (Cataract) by the refusal of the sectionmen and some others employed on the C.V.R. to proceed to work and after the heavy rains of Saturday and Sunday, the road was, in some places, blocked and trains unable to get through. Men were sent from Elora and elsewhere to take their places and upon reaching here were intimidated by the strikers and refused to work. Matters stood thus until about 5 o'clock when a compromise was reached and in two hours the line was clear and the first train dispatched from Toronto. The strikers numbered about forty men." The July 9th edition of the Brampton paper tells of a strike on the C.V.R. totally suspending traffic over the entire line due to wages in arrears as much as two months.

Whenever the Credit Valley is mentioned in writings of an historical nature, the borrowing of coal is always noted. Due to very tight money conditions, the officers were at their wits end trying to keep a supply of coal on hand for the use of their engines. Many times the Parkdale agent would be sent down to the Grand Trunk yard to induce the yardmen to put a loaded coal car on the interchange track. Soon this method of delivery came to a stop because the owners of the coal objected, and eventually the C.V.R. was hampered even to the extent of delaying passenger trains until arrangements could be made for coal to be sent up to the yards in horse-drawn carts. There it was shovelled into tenders of outgoing locomotives which would be standing coupled to cars with passengers aboard and ready to pull out. The coal owner was "Paddy" Burns of the famous Burns Coal Company of Toronto, one of the largest coal distributors in Ontario for years to come.

The October 20, 1881 edition of the "Canadian Champion" of Milton reads "A New Railroad - The Goderich people, growing tired of the monopoly enjoyed there by the Grand Trunk Railway are making overtures to the officials of the C.V.R. to induce them to build a branch of their road from Elora to Goderich, seventy miles distant and they offer a handsome bonus. If the proposals are not accepted, they will interview the directors of the Great Western or the Toronto, Grey and Bruce railways and see what terms can be made with them. Cause of hesitation on the part of the C.V.R. directors is the already large amount of debt on the road."

Shortly before the end of the year the inevitable rumours of sale or deals began to appear in the news. Again the Brampton "Conservator", taking an always active interest in the affairs of the C.V.R., came forth with an editorial on December 9, 1881 which observed "the air has been full of rumours for a fortnight of the sale of the Credit Valley first to the Great Western and next to the Canadian Pacific. Directors of the latter were interviewed at Montreal on Wednesday last about the report and state that they are not correct rumours but that negotiations are on foot by the C.P.R. syndicate to purchase or to lease both the Credit Valley and the Great Western Railways with a view to having stronger opposition through lines to the Great Trunk Railway. Furthermore we observe through advertisements in the "Mail" (Toronto) of yesterday that the Credit Valley Railway Company is making application to the Ontario Legislature to grant them in the next session power to amend their charter to extend their lines to London, Goderich, Berlin and other towns in the west, to lease their lines or parts of lines at present belonging to other companies and to lease their own lines to any other railway company should the C.V.R. see fit to do so. This last clause is the one to which every municipality that gave a dollar by way of bonus to the C.V.R. should stoutly object. The promises were made time and again by the directors of the C.V.R. that the road would be a competitive line and would be run in the interest of the people who were asked to pay large sums for its construction. To sell or lease this line to one of the powerful railway corporations such as the C.P. or the Great Western would be a betrayal of the peoples' confidence and rights and an act of gross treachery on behalf of the owners and directors of the road. Should it become known that any preliminary steps have been taken by the C.V.R. directors to transfer their interests to the C.P.R. or G.W.R. companies, meetings should be held by the councils of every municipality wherein bonuses were granted to the C.V.R. line and the most urgent protests entered against the transactions."

Such were the heated feelings of the Brampton paper, further borne out when one takes into consideration what these bonuses meant to the individual citizen at the time. In his book *Our Yesterdays* Andrew W. Taylor of Galt, when writing of the transportation in the area of Galt and Ayr, explains that "the bonus which the township gave to the company in 1874 raised the tax rate two and one half mills and, over a period of twenty years in the depressed '80s and early '90s proved a very irksome burden to the taxpayers."

Moving ahead to January 13, 1882, the Brampton "Conservator" ever alert, again reported under a title banner, "The Credit Valley Railway; the true inwardness of the lease by the Great Western: the Chicago Tribune of Saturday contains an article from the pen of a member of the staff who interviewed the general manager of the Great Western Railway at Eastwood on the first instance the purchase of the Credit Valley Railway by the Great Western Authorities. The information contained in the appended extract may be taken as officially correct. ' "The Great Western Railway has leased the Credit Valley road for 999 years, which runs from St. Thomas the central point of the Canada Southern, to Toronto. A company backed by the Great Western has been organized to build a line eastward from Toronto to a point of connection with the Canadian Pacific about a hundred and fifty miles west of the city of Montreal. At the commercial metropolis of Canada, it will connect with the Quebec, Montreal and Ottawa Road which in turn forms a close connection at Quebec with the Intercolonial road whose eastern terminus is Halifax. The Quebec, Montreal and Ottawa Road is the property of the government of the Province of Quebec and negotiations for its purchase by Sir Hugh Allen are now underway and it is understood in Canadian railway circles that this offer will be accepted. It was at first supposed that he was acting on behalf of the Grand Trunk people but later this was proved erroneous and information points conclusively that he is one of the Stevens-Osler-Childers syndicate between whom and the Grand Trunk there has not been any harmony for several months.'

"During the season of navigation for the past two years there has been an active rivalry between the Grand Trunk and the Great Western over the westbound immigrant business brought to Montreal by the Allen Steamship Line. The Great Western has also insisted that the Grand Trunk should divide the business west of Toronto which is the common junction point of the two systems in Western Canada and remain content with the absolute control of 330 miles of traffic. This the Grand Trunk refuses to do as the system touches all the important towns in Western Canada. In order to get any of the business, the Great Western was obliged to enter into an alliance with the steamboat lines running on Lake Ontario and the river St. Lawrence. This arrangement however was of value only during the season of navigation. When the boats ceased running on the Great Lakes, the whole of the traffic became the property of the Grand Trunk. The Great Western people admitted they would no longer submit; the Credit Valley road being in the market, they wisely took it in so as to prevent it falling into the hands of the Grand Trunk and having thus, two lines from the Michigan Frontier to Toronto, they came to the conclusion that they were in a position to force the fight on the Grand Trunk. To aid in this direction, they joined hands with the Canadian Pacific syndicate and the indications are that before the

year has lapsed, there will be a well-built line running through the thickly
settled farm country and close enough to the Grand Trunk for a distance of
330 miles, to give it as keen a competition as it may desire. It is also
understood that as soon as Sir Hugh Allen acquires the Quebec, Montreal
and Ottawa Road, he will make Quebec the summer terminus of the Allan
Steamship Line, the inland business of which will be given to the Q. M. and
Ottawa Railway. The Michigan Central will connect Chicago with this new
Canadian line to the Seaboard."

The fight for survival now joined, the Ontario and Quebec Railway
came into being, and serious meetings began to take place to settle the
Credit Valley Railway's position. It was at this precise moment that the
Credit Valley became the Third Giant: the key to entry into the Toronto
market as well as the long finger joining the United States market through
St. Thomas with the proposed connection with the C.P.R., namely the Ontario and Quebec Railway. The route for the C.V.R. chosen by George
Laidlaw, though ostensibly patterned from finance rather than engineering
and foresight, gave the Canadian Pacific Railway the key to transprovincial
routing which has yet to be equalled by its rival the C.N.R.

The final entry by the Brampton "Conservator" is a stroke of reporting
genius. It is quoted here to fill two purposes; first, it records the method of
the ending of the Credit Valley Railway's brief claim to fame, and second, it
pays a short but glowing tribute to the railway's promoter, George Laidlaw:

The Brampton "Conservator", November 23, 1883
The Credit Valley Railway

At the adjourned meeting of the shareholders of the Credit
Valley Railway yesterday, it was decided to lease the London
Junction Railway for 999 years at the price of $18,800 per year and
also to amalgamate with the Ontario and Quebec Railway. At the
adjourned meeting of the shareholders of the Ontario and Quebec
Railway, it was decided to make several extensive additions to the
line. The Toronto "World", November 20th refers to the incident -
'The amalgamation of the Credit Valley with the Ontario and
Quebec was consumated yesterday at a meeting of the former
company. Mr. Osler was there with proxies for the majority of the
stock and he had the little motions drawn and ready for sub-
mission. It passed without opposition and the Credit Valley
Railway was wiped out of existence as a Toronto concern and
passed into the hands of the C.P.R. without a murmur. The last of
the railways promoted by the King of the Bonus Hunters, George
Laidlaw, and which were ever to remain independent, surrendered

without a shot from that remarkable man. The consolidation now
includes the Toronto, Grey and Bruce, the Credit Valley and the
Ontario and Quebec; the headquarters of which will be in the old
U.E. building on King St. and before long the Northern will join
the consolidation despite the denials of the Hamilton "Times".
When that is consumated, everything will have been gobbled up
by the two great gobblers and the only thing left them to fight over
is the Kingston Tramway.

**Canadian Pacific Railway Construction Crew filling in the Forks of the
Credit Trestle 1884;** *Vincent X. McEnaney photo*

And so the history of the Credit Valley comes to an end:
Born February 15, 1871,
Died November 20, 1883

But such was the vision of George Laidlaw that even today, as this is
written, the entire trackage of the railway, save a small section of some three
miles from Melville into the terminus at Orangeville, is still in use as the
main line of the Canadian Pacific Railway. From Streetsville to Orangeville
and thence northward to Owen Sound and the Georgian Bay area; from
Cataract west to Elora; from Toronto through Streetsville to St. Thomas
and thence west to Windsor and Detroit, these are the main lines of the
C.P.R.

EPILOGUE

In the spring of 1971 a group or railway enthusiasts joined together to bring back to life the steam giants of yesteryear. After much searching, they were successful in obtaining a steam locomotive which could conceivably be repaired and made operational.

It is one thing to obtain a locomotive, rebuild it and make it available for display. Many such locomotives, with assorted passenger cars, are to be found on private "tourist type" rail lines in Canada and the U.S., however, these men, visionaries like George Laidlaw, decided that although they would like to have their own trackage on which to run their train, they would require a method of creating profits within their enterprise, if ever it were to be successful. Their engine, and its train, must be brought up to the standards of safety as required by the Department of Transportation so that it could be operated over any trackage of any railway in North America. This was the challenge that they chose for themselves. They began to enlist the help, both physical and financial, of as many businesses as possible.

With the help of the Canadian Pacific Railway, the locomotive was housed in the John Street roundhouse in Toronto and a general overhaul was begun. Railway "old-timers" began to appear, who with their skills, and the enthusiasm of the youthful members, slowly began to dismantle the locomotive. To ensure the ultimate success that the membership was striving for, the job was done painstakingly slow but, as has been finally proven, their methods were correct. The locomotive required complete retubing before its boilers could be certified as safe. It became necessary to again enlist the aid of "old-time" experts to renew the trades they had practised in the days of steam. Slowly the locomotive began to reappear as a shiny black powerhouse.

Meanwhile the coal and water-carrying tender began to have repairs made, and, when completed, it was remarried to the newly rebuilt locomotive. Thus on May 19, 1973, emerged #1057, an ex-C.P.R. ten-wheeler, resplendent in gleaming black, with white trim and glistening

Credit Valley Railway excursion train near Inglewood - 1973; *Author's photo*

Engine 1057 of the Credit Valley Railway at Cataract 1973; *Author's photo*

nickel and brass. She bore the name 'Credit Valley' on her side and she awaited the completion of the balance of the rolling stock which she would proudly lead across the province.

At the car shops in Hamilton and in Toronto, other members rebuilt the passenger cars generously donated by the railways. There are those of the membership that would challenge the statement that these cars were operational equipment when received, since it seemed that at every turn of the hammer and saw, new obstacles appeared to hinder the progress of repair. Like their brothers-in-arms in the locomotive department, they persevered, and suddenly their efforts culminated in the appearance of a complete train of tuscan red passenger cars. They too proudly bore the name 'Credit Valley' and the members chose to name their equipment after the many hamlets on the Credit River through which the cars would travel. It now only required the joining up of locomotive - tender and passenger cars to make a train. The first major challenge had been overcome; the next was now to appear. Could this railway be made operational? Indeed, it was a railway; it is constituted as a railway and to *be* a railway it is necessary to have a train and to operate it.

While all the reconditioning was going on, other members became active in the publicity and public relations arenas. Membership drives brought in new faces; newspapers provided public exposure, and the continuous drive of the enthusiastic core of "railfans" finally caught the eye of the local politicians. A major breakthrough was about to occur. Together with the possibility of obtaining an unused section of the Canadian National Railway trackage between Georgetown and Cheltenham, the executive of the newly formed railway began to open negotiations with the Township of Chinguacousy to settle their headquarters in the latest "toy" of the Township, Cheltenham Park.

In order to have a proper railway terminal, it is necessary to have locomotive and car repair buildings, and since this is a steam railway, a turntable is a necessity. Where does a turntable come from in this day of diesels? A new table was out of the question due to cost, but at the end of the Elora-Fergus branch of the C.P.R. (originally the C.V.R.) was an unused and abandoned turntable. Again the membership rallied, and fortunately for all concerned, one of the members happened to be the president of a construction company. So it came to pass that cranes and flatbed trucks appeared in Elora, after C.P.R. permission had been obtained, and an old turntable was raised out of its pit, placed on a flatbed trailer, and trucked about thirty miles to its new site at Cheltenham Park.

As publicity began to appear, the interest of railfans across the continent began to appear also. An opening run of a brand new railway was imminent. The official car of the parent organization, Ontario Rail, was chosen as the tail-end passenger car to officially complete the first run of the Credit Valley Railway. Interest on behalf of the Canadian Pacific Railway was indicated by the insertion of the private car of the General Manager of the railway into the train as it made its inaugural trip.

It was obvious that the new Credit Valley Railway should open its doors to members and railfans; the success of the first trip was overwhelming. The train was sold out months before it was to run, and when the trip was finally made on May 27, 1973, it was a tremendous success for all concerned. The train was met at every crossing, at every station, at every bridge, in fact at every vantage point, by hundreds of spectators, many of whom had never seen a steam train in operation before. Cameras were everywhere and #1057 became a "star".

The new Credit Valley Railway "highballing" past Cheltenham Siding on it's inaugural run May 27, 1973; *Author's photo*

"It is said that the lasting memorial to the steam locomotive lies not in statistics, nor upon the printed page, or even on museum grounds. It is in the hearts and minds of all who saw and heard the iron horse in action. The smoke of their last going saddened the hearts of all that had known and loved them.

. . . And yet it is possible to recapture some of this enchantment, this charisma of the steam age.

To this end the Ontario Rail Association is dedicated."

ACKNOWLEDGEMENTS

The author wishes to express his thanks to the following, who provided photographs, information, advice and encouragement to bring this volume to its ultimate form.

Mrs. Jean Shields - Coboconk (Grandaughter of George Laidlaw)

Mr. Ralph Beaumont - Mississauga

Mr. Maurice Boyd - Toronto

Mr. Andrew Merrillees - Toronto

Mrs. Ethel Stone, Curator, Wellington County Historical Museum - Elora

Mr. Omer Lavallee, Public Relations, Canadian Pacific Railway - Montreal, P.Q.

Miss Elizabeth Willmot - Toronto

Mr. David E. Ross - Toronto

Miss Elizabeth Colley, Librarian, Streetsville Public Library - Streetsville

Mr. S.W. Walker - Toronto

Mrs. B. Matheson - Orangeville

Mr. K. Pinkney - Caledon

Mrs. G. Barber - Orangeville

Mr. V.X. McEnaney - Toronto

Mr. A.M. McKitrick - Ottawa

Mr. D. Spalding - Toronto

Mr. C. Smeaten - Inglewood

Mr. J. Lock - Brampton

Mr. W. Roulston, Librarian, Brampton Public Library - Brampton

Mr. R.B. Lackey - Orangeville

Mrs. Mary Manning - Streetsville

Mr. Regis Yaworski - Brampton

Mr. John Kessel - Brampton

Mr. Roy Downs - Milton

Mr. Edward Boss - McMurray, Pennsylvania

Mrs. Mildred Belleghem - Mississauga

Ralph Beaumont deserves special mention because of his untiring efforts tracking down hundreds of sources. His particular interest is hereby recognized and appreciated.

James F. Filby
Boston Mills, Ontario

APPENDIX

Mainline — Toronto to St. Thomas

Mile (from Toronto)	Feature	Elevation (feet above Lake Ont)
0	Toronto — Union Station	0
1.9	Start of main line, Junction with Grand Trunk	50
2.25	Parkdale Station	58
2.3	Steel Girder (2) Bridge	60
2.4	Siding to Rubber Factory	62
3.2	Dundas St.	100
4.5	West Toronto Junction	146
6.6	Lambton Station	152
7.4	Humber River	151
8.6	Mimico River	150
8.75	Islington Station (Flag)	155
11.6	Etobicoke River	128
12.2	Pallet Creek	128
12.8	Dixie Station (Flag)	126
14.25	Cooksville Station	144
14.3	Siding to Gravel Pit	144
14.8	Trestle Bridge	153
17.5	Springfield Station (Flag)	229
19.7	Barber's Ravine	246
20	Credit River	246
20.4	Trestle Bridge	251
20.5	Streetsville Station	253
21.7	Streetsville Junction Station	303
21.8	Pile Bridge	299
22.1	Pile Bridge	299
23	Trestle Bridge	343
24.8	Boundary between Toronto & Trafalgar Twps.	426
25	Trafalgar Station (Flag)	437
27.7	Hornby Station (Flag)	402
28.2	Iron Girder Bridge	386
28.4	Pile Bridge	380
28.7	Pile Bridge	376

96.6	Pile Bridge	630
97	Ingersol Station	628
100	Siding to Gravel Pit	654
100.6	Boundary between Oxford & Middlesex Cty.	643
102	Putnam Station	644
102.9	Reynolds Creek	626
104	Pine Creek	692
106.6	Harrietsville Station	700
111.1	Boundary between Middlesex and Elgin Cty.	637
111.5	Kettle Creek	618
112.4	Boundary between South Dorchester & Yarmouth	599
112.8	Belmont Station	599
113.9	Catfish Creek	565
117.6	Salt Creek	546
120.1	Great Western Railway Crossing	538
120.9	Snow Plough Siding	530
121	St. Thomas Station, junction with Michigan Central Railroad	527

Orangeville Branch — Streetsville to Orangeville

21.5	Streetsville Junction Station	316
23.5	Meadowville Station (S. of Derry Rd.)	316
23.75	Howe Truss Bridge (N. of Derry Rd.)	316
24.75	Credit River — Howe Truss Bridge	313
26	Churchville Station (Flag)	357
26.25	Trestle Bridge (N. of Town Line)	357
27.1	Crossing Con. Rd. 2 & 3 Chinguacousy	427
28.2	Crossing Con. Rd. 1 & 2 W. Chinguacousy	449
28.4	Trestle Bridge — Fletchers Creek	460
29	Brampton Station	474
29.4	Grand Trunk Railway Crossing	460
31	Road Lots 10 & 11	520
32.9	Road allowance Lots 15 & 16	558
33.75	Edmonton Station (Flag) ½M. W. of Snelgrove	591
34.9	Trestle Bridge — Approx. Lot 20	609
35.5	Trestle Bridge — Lot 22 n Con. 1 W. & Hurontario	622
35.8	Road allowance Lot 22 & 23	634
36.2	Trestle Bridge — Between Con. 1 W. & Hurontario	647
36.6	Trestle Bridge	665
37.1	Road Allowance Con. 1 & 2	683
37.75	Road Lots 27 & 28 Flag Station	694
38.4	Road Allowance Con. 2 & 3	690

38.75	Cheltenham Station (Flag)	690
39.8	Trestle Bridge — ¼M. N. Cheltenham Stn., Rd.	676
40.3	Trestle Bridge — Rd. Allowance Con. 2 & 3	661
40.5	Rd. allowance Lot 32-33 (Boston Mills)	651
41.1	Credit River Bridge — Just N. of Townline Road	629
41.6	Inglewood Station — Jct. N.&N.W. Railway	642
42.9	Trestle Bridge	710
43.2	Trestle Bridge	728
43.3	Con. Rd. 1 & 2W Caledon	733
43.5	Trestle Bridge	742
44.3	Con. Rd. 2 & 3W, Caledon	781
45.2	Trestle Bridge	781
45.5	Forks of Credit Trestle — W. Branch Credit River	833
45.7	Forks of Credit Station (Flag)	833
46	Trestle Bridge	854
46.2	Rd. Allow. Lots 10 & 11; Caledon	866
47	Trestle Bridge	914
47.2	Trestle Bridge — South of Church's Mills	962
47.9	Rd. Allow. Con. 3 & 4	980
48.3	Cataract Station (Church's Falls) Junction of Elora Branch	1000
49	Trestle Bridge	1050
51	Road Lots 22-23	1068
51.2	Alton Station	1066
51.7	Trestle Bridge — over Credit River tributary	1049
52.5	Road Allow. Con. 2 & 3	1066
52.8	Howe Truss Bridge — Credit River S. of Melville	1066
53.3	Crossing T.G.&B. Railway	1078
53.4	Melville Junction	1078
53.7	Trestle Bridge — Credit River N. of Con. Rd.	1074
55.1	Trestle Bridge — Credit River Con. 1W Caledon	1084
55.8	Trestle Bridge — Credit River Con. 1W Caledon	1081
56.4	Town Line Con. 1 W. Caledon	1000
56.7	Orangeville Station	1000
56.8	End of Rail	1000

Elora Branch — Cataract to Elora

0	Cataract Station (Church's Falls)	1004
0.6	Church's Siding	1035
0.7	Road Allow. Con. 3 & 4 Caledon	1035
0.9	Road Allow. Cataract to 4th Con.	1030
1	Con. Road 4 & 5 Caledon	1034

2.1	Nineveh Siding Con. Rds. 5 & 6	1049
2.8	Gravel Pit Siding — Con. 6 Caledon	1060
3.5	Trestle Bridge — N. Branch of West Credit River	1037
3.7	Con. Rd. 10 & 11 Erin Twp.	1039
4.3	Con. Rd. 9 & 10 Erin Twp.	1044
4.7	Erin Station	1044
5.4	Road Allow. Lots 17 & 18 Con. 9 Erin	1050
5.7	Con. Rd. 8 & 9 Erin	1065
7.7	Road Allow. Lots 20 & 21 Con. 8 Erin Twp.	1154
8	Road Allow. Con. 7 & 8, Erin Twp.	1154
8.1	Trestle Bridge — West Credit River Lot 22 Con. 7	1160
8.3	Hillsburg Station	1169
8.7	Gravel Pit	1190
9	Con. Road 6 & 7	1202
9.5	Pile Bridge — Lot 24, Con. 6, Erin	1198
10.1	Con. Road 5 & 6	1205
10.8	Road Allow. Lots 27 & 28	1212
11.1	Con. Road 4 & 5	1211
13	Orton Station (Flag)	1202
13.1	Trestle Bridge	1203
15	Road Allow. Lots 5 & 6 East Garafraxa Twp.	1281
15.1	Con. Road 9 & 10 East Garafraxa Twp.	1281
16.3	Con. Road 8 & 9 East Garafraxa Twp.	1215
17.5	Con. Road 7 & 8 East Garafraxa	1167
17.6	Belwood Station (Douglas) Con. 7 East Garafraxa	1167
18	Trestle Bridge	1153
18.5	Con. Road 6 & 7	1118
18.8	Grand River Con. 6 West Garafraxa Trestle Bridge	1118
19.3	Con. Road 5 & 6 West Garafraxa Twp.	1121
20.3	Con. Road 4 & 5	1136
20.6	Spires Station (Flag)	1143
20.8	Trestle Bridge	1143
21.2	Con. Road 3 & 4	1154
22	Spires Station Relocation 1939	1153
22.1	Con. Road 2 & 3	1153
22.8	Con. Road 1 & 2	1153
23.9	Trestle Bridge Con. 1 West Garafraxa	1128
24.7	Crossing of Hamilton & Northwestern	1113
25	Fergus Station	1100
26.7	Road Allow. Lots 12 & 13	1084
27.3	McMahons Siding Con. 12 Nichol Twp.	1047
27.5	Elora Station Con. 11, Nichol Twp.	1047

(margin label spanning rows 18.5–21.2: Belwood Lake)

BIBLIOGRAPHY

Trout, J.M. & Edw. - The Railways of Canada, Monetary Times, Toronto, 1871

Taylor, Conyngham Crawford - Toronto Called Back, from 1892 to 1847, William Briggs, Toronto, 1892

Constable, T.A. - Canada and its Provinces, 1914

Constable, T.A. - History of Peel County: Township of Chinguacousy History, Charters Publishing, Brampton, 1967

Mulvany, C. Pelham - Toronto Past and Present until 1882

Price, Alfred - George Laidlaw, Pioneer Railway Builder, The Canadian Magazine, Vol. 67-68, Dec. 1927

Smith, W.H. - Canada: Past, Present and Future, 1852

Guillet, Edwin C. - Early Life in Upper Canada, Ontario Publishing Co. Ltd., Toronto, 1933

City of Toronto - Special Committee Report - Ald. McMurrich, Chairman, March 5, 1880

Grant, George Munroe - Picturesque Canada, Vol. 2, Toronto, 1882

Hutchinson, Jean F. - West Garafraxa Township Centennial Guide - 1967

Centennial Committee - Erin Township and Erin Village Centennial History - 1967

Farrell, Dr. Marian A. - The Guelph Junction Railway (1884-1950 - 1951

Shanley, Frank - Report of Mr. Frank Shanley, Prepared by Order of the Railway Committee of the Privy Council and the Decision of the Railway Committee Thereon - Toronto, 1879

Author Unknown - The History of Boston Mills, From a paper given November 19, 1946

Leming, Isabell - The Caledon Comment, Vo. 8, No. 4 - The Caledon Hills Bruce Trail Club - 1971

Price, Alfred - Credit Valley Memoirs, Canadian Pacific Railway - 1926

The Historical Atlas of York County

The Etobicoke Press, August 11, 1955, Page 11

Givens, John - The Story of Etobicoke

Carson, Jo - Womens Photos of Railway Stations, Miss Elizabeth Willmot - Toronto Globe and Mail, May 20, 1971

Glazebrook, G.p.de - Transportation in Canada - Vol. 2
Blake, V.B. - 1957 Conservation Report Chapter 8 & 9, Credit Valley Conservation Authority, 1957
Bromley, John F. and Filey, Mike - Rails from the Junction: the Story of The Toronto Suburban Railway
Bromley, John F. and Filey, Mike - Farewell to Steam in Canada
Bull, Perkins - From Macdonnell to McGuigan, The Perkins Bull Foundation, Toronto, 1936
Smith's Canadian Gazetteer, Canada West 1846, H. & W. Boswell, Toronto, 1846
Centennial Committee - Brampton Centennial Souvenir, C.V. Charters, Brampton, 1953
Kerr, Donald and Spelt, Jacob - The Changing Face of Toronto
Heyes, Esther - The Story of Albion: From Caledon to Vaughan, 1961
The Brampton Times, 1971
The Brampton Conservator, 1871 to 1884 inclusive
The Orangeville Banner
The Orangeville Sun
The Milton Canadian Champion
Brown, J.J. - The Inventors, The Canadian Illustrated Library, Toronto, 1967
Laidlaw, George - Reports and Letters on Light Narrow Gauge Railways, Globe Printing, Toronto, 1867
Clark, Gwen - Halton's Pages of the Past, Dill's Printing and Publishing Co., Acton 1955

PICTURE CREDITS

Public Archives of Ontario   pg. 35 68 70 73
Vincent X. McEnaney   pg. 46 81 82 94
"Chummy" Smeaton   pg. 36 38 39
Edgar Ireland   pg. 67
Ralph Beaumont   pg. 66
Mrs. William Russell   pg. 72 75
James Filby   pg. 65 96 98
Mrs. Jean Sheilds   pg. 20 23 25 26
Public Archives of Canada   pg. 11
C.P.R.   pg. 6 85
Toronto Public Library   pg. 33 41 52 54 57 74
Mrs. M. Belleghem   pg. 48 61

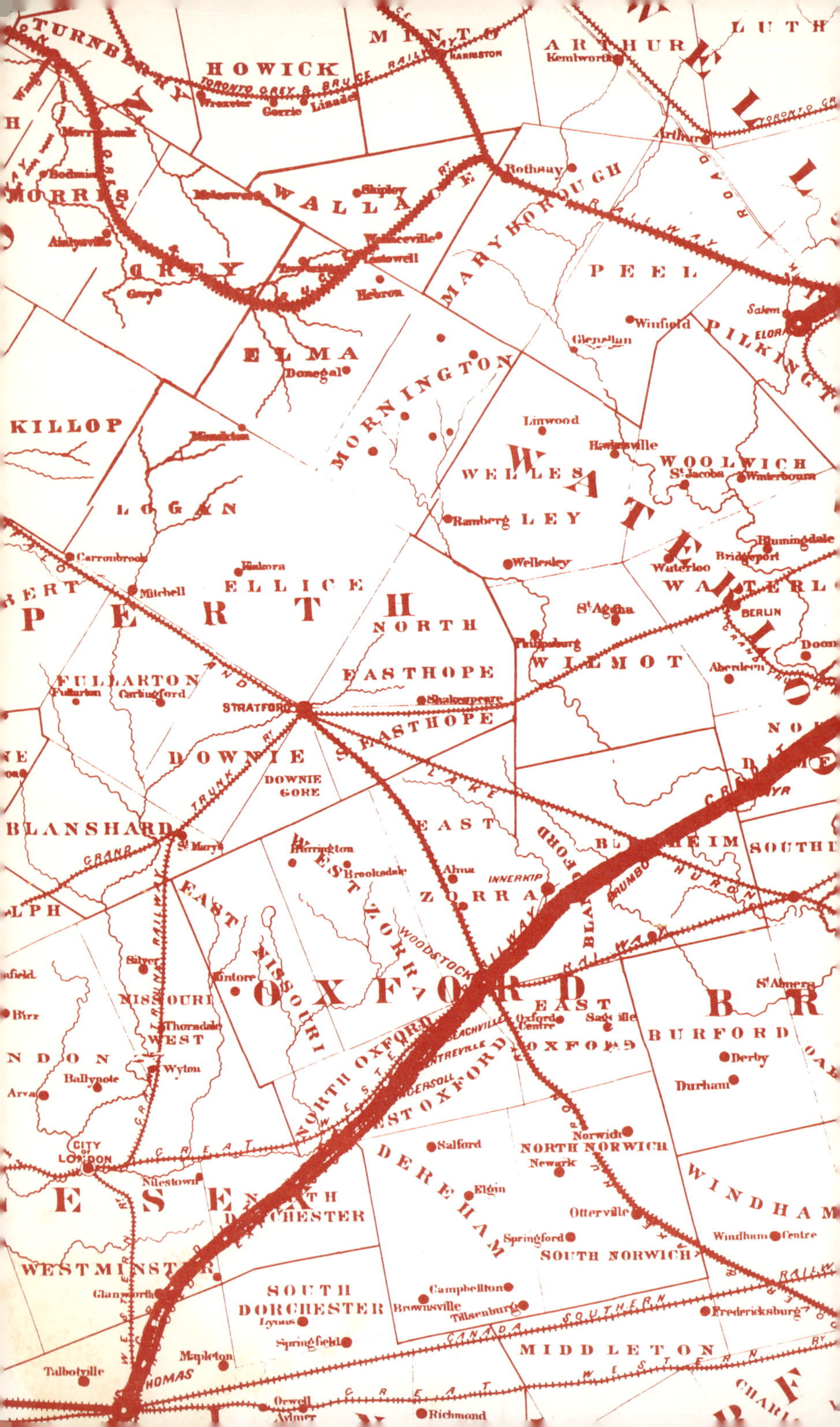

TURNBERRY
HOWICK
MINTO
ARTHUR
LUTH
Kenilworth
WELLI
Wroxeter
Gorrie Lisadel
Harriston
TORONTO GREY & BRUCE RAILWAY
TORONTO G
MORRIS
Bodmin
Belmore
Shipley
WALLACE
Rothsay
MARYBOROUGH
PEEL
PILKINGT
Ainlayville
Gowanstown
Listowel
Arthur
RAILWAY
ROAD
Salem
GREY
Gowrie
Hebron
Glenallan
Winfield
ELORA
KILLOP
Donegal
ELMA
MORNINGTON
Linwood
Hawkesville
WOOLWICH
St Jacobs Winterbourne
LOGAN
WELLES
LEY
Rambers
WATER
Bloomingdale
Bridgeport
Carronbrook
Hakora
ELLICE
Wellesley
Waterloo
WATERL
Mitchell
PERTH
St Agatha
BERLIN
NORTH
Philipsburg
Doon
FULLARTON
EASTHOPE
WILMOT
Aberdeen
Fullarton Carlingford
Shakespeare
STRATFORD
NO
DOWNIE
EASTHOPE
DALM
DOWNIE
GORE
AYR
BLANSHARD
EAST
LAKE
BLENHEIM
SOUTH
St Marys
GRAND
Harrington
WEST
Brookdale
Alma
INNERKIP
HURON
LPH
Silver
 Embro
ZORRA
EAST
NISSOURI
Kintore
OXFORD
WOODSTOCK
St Almers
Birr
NISSOURI
EAST
BR
Arva
Thorndale
WEST
Oxford
Centre
Sackville
BURFORD
NDON
Ballymote
Wyton
NORTH OXFORD
WEST OXFORD
Derby
Ingersoll
EAST OXFORD
Durham
CITY
of
LONDON
Beachville
Centreville
Nilestown
Salford
Norwich
NORTH NORWICH
WINDHAM
DEREHAM
Newark
ESEX
NORTH
DORCHESTER
Elgin
Otterville
Windham Centre
Springford
WESTMINSTER
SOUTH NORWICH
SOUTH
DORCHESTER
Campbellton
Glanworth
Brownsville
Lyons
Tillsonburg
Fredericksburg
SOUTHERN
CANADA
MIDDLETON
Springfield
Mapleton
Talbotville
THOMAS
GREAT
WESTERN
RAILWAY
Orwell
Aylmer
Richmond
CHAR